THE LAST REVIEW

THE LAST REVIEW
The Confederate Reunion, Richmond, 1932

by
Virginius Dabney

and including "The Last Parade"
by Douglas Southall Freeman

Algonquin Books
1984

LIBRARY OF CONGRESS CATALOGING IN PUBLICATION DATA
Dabney, Virginius, 1901–   . The last review.
Bibliography: p.   Includes index.
1. United States—History—Civil War, 1861–1865—
Anniversaries, etc. 2. Confederate States of America.
Army—Anniversaries, etc. 3. Richmond (Va.)—History—
Civil War, 1861–1865—Anniversaries, etc.   I. Freeman,
Douglas Southall, 1886–1953.   The last parade. 1984. II. Title
E548.D33 1984   973.7′6   84-337 ISBN 0-912697-06-7

ALGONQUIN BOOKS
P.O. Box 2225, Chapel Hill, N.C. 27515–2225

For
Alice and Johnny
with Love

Contents

Acknowledgments

I should like first of all to express my indebtedness to John D. Beall, DDS, of Richmond, who made available to us a copy of the program for the 1896 Reunion, the sixth such, from which we were able to photograph not only several pictures appearing in the text of this volume, but the handsome color drawings that appear on the dust jacket. Dr. Beall also permitted us to photograph the first-day postal cachet for the Reunion which appears herein.

I am indebted for assistance with this book to Louis D. Rubin, Jr., president of Algonquin Books, who suggested the work and was of much help in its writing and editing. George Core also was of great assistance with the editing. The accounts and photographs of the 1932 Confederate Reunion, published in the *Richmond Times-Dispatch* and *News Leader*, were essential sources. The papers' Reference Department was always helpful, notably Charles Saunders, Larry Hall, Kathy Albers, Elva Blanton, and John Clarke. In the Photographic Department P. A. Gormus, Jr., and Joanne Slough gave generous assistance. Roland Galvin performed an inestimable service in informing me that there was a scrapbook at the Museum of the Confederacy containing much of the material that we were seeking. The museum cooperated handsomely in allowing us to photograph its contents. We are indebted especially to Cathy Carlson and Elizabeth Scott McKemie in this connection, and also to Edward D. C. Campbell, Jr., who is now with the Virginia Historical Society. Virginius C. Hall, Jr., of that Society, also was most cooperative. At the Valentine Museum we were assisted greatly by John G. Zehmer, Jr., Sarah Shields, and Tucker Hill. Robert and Elisabeth Dementi of Dementi-Foster Studios were in every way helpful. The staff of the Virginia State Library, notably Louis Manarin, placed us in their debt, as did the staff of the Richmond Public Library.

For permission to reprint in facsimile the issue of *Richmond Magazine* for June, 1932, which served as the official program of the Reunion, we are indebted to the Richmond Chamber of Commerce.

It seemed fitting to include in this book the full text and illustrations of the late Douglas Southall Freeman's "The Last Parade." Originally published as an editorial in the *Richmond News Leader* for June 24, 1932, it aroused such favorable comment that it was subsequently printed in a handsome edition, for private distribution only, by Whittet and Shepperson of Richmond, with tipped-in photographs of the monuments along the parade route. To the best of our knowledge it has not until now been made available to the general reading public. For its use we are indebted to Dr. Freeman's daughter, Mrs. Leslie Cheek, Jr., the former Mary Tyler Freeman, of Richmond.

Thanks for other items and for assistance in the preparation of this volume go to Marion H. Giannafi, of the United Daughters of the Confederacy headquarters staff, and to C. Hobson Goddin, Samuel J. T. Moore, Jr., Lucille S. Lacy, Wilbur L. Jenkins, Jr., Robert T. Barton, III, Lee A. Wallace, Jr., Ivy Engard, James I. Robertson, Jr. Bernard J. Henley, William F. Mallory, and Major General William D. McKain.

The lines from Allen Tate's "To the Lacedemonians" are reprinted by permission of Farrar, Straus and Giroux, Inc. They are excerpted from an early version of the poem, which in its final form appears in *Collected Poems 1919–1976* by Allen Tate, © 1936, 1977 by Allen Tate.

VIRGINIUS DABNEY

Richmond, Virginia
September 20, 1983

I

THE LAST REVIEW: A MEMOIR

**First-day cachet for 1932 Reunion, with two-cent
Confederate and United States postage stamps,
sponsored by Richmond Stamp Club.**
Courtesy John D. Beall.

The Last Review: A Memoir

Hundreds of white-haired and grizzled old men who fought long years before at Spotsylvania's Bloody Angle or the siege of Vicksburg, rode with Forrest's daring cavalry, or wrote their names on history's scroll in Pickett's charge at Gettysburg gathered for their forty-second and last major reunion in June, 1932, at Richmond, the once-beleaguered capital of the Confederate States of America.

They were in their eighties and nineties, most of them too feeble to walk in the parades, a goodly number with a missing leg or empty sleeve. A fifteen-year-old drummer boy who enlisted near the end of the war was eighty-two in 1932. Nearly all of the fifteen hundred Confederate veterans who came to Richmond for the reunion on seven special trains from throughout the South were older than that.

I was a reporter for the *Richmond Times-Dispatch* when the last great reunion took place, more than fifty years ago. As the veterans began arriving in town I was sent out to the Old Soldiers' Home to describe the scene. Confederate veterans were a well-remembered part of my youth when I was growing up at the University of Virginia. I saw them there in dwindling numbers, members of the Charlottesville camp of the United Confederate Veterans, who were on hand each Memorial Day at the University Cemetery, where many were buried. I recall especially the inscription on the Confederate monument which stood amid the graves: "Fate Denied Them Victory But Clothed Them With Glorious Immortality."

My grandfather, for whom I am named, was a captain on the staff of General John B. Gordon. He was wounded at Second Manassas, and carried the ball in his body for the rest of his life. When he recovered from his wound he went back into action, and fought on until the surrender at Appomattox. My father, Richard Heath Dabney, a Heidelberg Ph.D. who taught history at the University of Virginia for forty-nine years and was dean of the graduate school for eighteen of those years, adored his father. "No braver man ever went into battle," he once said to me. As a student in Germany in the 1880s, Father told a gathering that he was glad the South had lost the war. Later he expressed deep regret that he had made this statement, since he felt that it reflected on his father and the cause for which he had risked his life. Certainly my father instilled in me an appreciation of the bravery and fortitude shown by the men and women of the South both during and after the war. In fact our somewhat scruffy carriage horse was named for Wade Hampton. As a boy of about six I asked Father who Wade Hampton was, and he explained that Hampton was a famous Confederate general.

It was with this heritage and rearing that I visited the Old Soldiers' Home during the convention of 1932, as a reporter for the *Times-Dispatch*.

I was moved by the sight of the old warriors sitting under the trees. The Confederate tradition was in my bones. Not only my grandfather for whom I am named, but my other grandfather, James M. M. Davis, of the Rockbridge Artillery, had fought for the Confederacy, not to mention various other near relatives. Yet at the same time it was apparent to me that while admiration for the brave men who had gone into battle for a cause in which they believed was distinctly in order, we of the modern generation should not spend our time looking backward and dwelling excessively on the past glories of the old plantation South.

Vanguard of Veterans Arrive for Forty-Second Annual Reunion

Texas Colonel Relates How Accident Caused His Capture

Tall but true tales are told by many of the survivors of the Confederate Army. Stories of heroic deeds, reminiscences of the great leaders, amusing camp incidents—these are overheard in hotel lobbies, at the encampments, everywhere that two or three men in gray are assembled.

But few stories can equal the thrilling experiences of Colonel Edward C. Wilson of Electra, Texas. Colonel Wilson enlisted at the outbreak of the war in the Louisiana regiment of which his father was a captain and his three brothers members. He was detailed to spy duty, and disguised as a Negro produce vender, was successful in bringing back valuable information to his soldiers. In his bandana, calico dress and apron, he ventured into a Union officer's tent, and

a Yankee soldier slapped him for his audacity. The blow brushed off some of the charcoal which begrimed his face and he was straitway clapped into prison.

Escaping, he rejoined his regiment and fought with his father and brothers at the Battle of Gettysburg. Captured again, he obtained a parole to search on the field for one of his brothers whom he had seen fall in a rout. His search disclosed the bullet-ridden bodies of all three brothers and of his father. Such tragedy affected even the hearts of enemy officers, and he was permitted an extension of parole to accompany the bodies back home for burial.

Returning, he surrendered to the Yankee officers and successfully made his escape a short while later.

Upper left shows Governor Pollard, center, and a group of veterans and sponsors witnessing the raising of the Confederate flag on the Capitol. On his right are a sponsor, General DeSassure; Dr. George R. Tabor, commander-in-chief, S. C. V., Walter L. Hopkins, adjutant and chief of staff, S. C. V. Oval to right, shows General DeSassure and General W. B. Freeman of Richmond. Center left shows, among others, Dr. Tabor, Mr. Hopkins, Charles T. Norman of Richmond. Center right, two officers of the Richmond Blues and sponsors. Below, in the oval, is shown the first veterans to get off the DeSassure train at Broad Street Station. Lower right, a shot from the Capitol roof, showing the Stars and Bars being raised.

—From the Richmond Times-Dispatch.

In the late nineteenth century, when the wrecked and bleeding states of the former Confederacy were struggling to recover from the effects of their defeat, many Southerners viewed the antebellum scene through a sort of golden haze. A typical example of this undiscerning nostalgia, combined with opposition to virtually all modern advances, can be seen in an address delivered in 1891 by Charles Colcock Jones, Jr., of Georgia, whose history of that state led the historian George Bancroft to hail him as "the Macaulay of the South."

Under the absurd guise of a new South, flaunting the banners of utilitarianism—lifting the standards of speculation and expediency—elevating the colors whereon are emblazoned consolidation of wealth and centralization of government—lowering the flag of intellectual, moral and refined supremacy in the presence of the petty guidons of ignorance, personal ambition and diabolism—supplanting the iron cross with the golden calf . . . ; and careless of the landmarks of the fathers, impatient of the restraints of a calm, enlightened conservative civilization, viewing with an indifferent eye the tokens of Confederate valor, and slighting the graves of the Confederate dead, would counsel no oblation save at the shrine of Mammon.

Such jeremiads were being heard less and less in the first third of the twentieth century, and this was cause for rejoicing. It was one thing to honor the memory of those who had defended the South from the invader, many at the cost of their lives. It was something else to indulge in indiscriminate praise of everything in the antebellum era, and to let the Lost Cause dominate one's thinking, thus preventing one from going forward into the new day with new ideas and new challenges.

In 1932 Richmond and the rest of the South were moving out of the atmosphere of despair and defeat induced by such a poem as Father Ryan's "The Conquered Banner." And yet even then there were those who looked to the past, and were unable to view the issues involved in the conflict of the 1860s with anything like detachment. Only a short time before I went out to the Soldiers' Home during the reunion, I had been shocked by the reaction of a Richmond audience to a quotation from Abraham Lincoln which Albert Bushnell

Hart of the Harvard faculty had included in an address in the city. The quotation was not anti-Southern in the slightest degree, but as the meeting broke up several persons remarked that Hart had showed execrable taste in quoting Lincoln at all.

Such attitudes have become increasingly rare in Richmond and the South generally, until today it is doubtful if any such remark would be heard in the region. For one thing, most Southerners now believe that Lincoln was favorably disposed toward the South after the war, and that the former Confederacy would have fared much better during the Reconstruction if he had lived. More than that, however, the passionate loyalties and hatreds of the Civil War period and the Reconstruction have subsided. Sectional consciousness no doubt remains, but as those who fought in and remembered the war passed away, so did the intense emotions that had characterized their time and place. Thus that last Confederate reunion in Richmond in 1932 symbolized the close of an era of Southern history and a phase of sectional consciousness.

The Richmond where the aged veterans were assembling bore numerous signs, in the form of heroic statuary, of the reverence in which the Lost Cause was held in the generations following the war. During the late nineteenth century and well into the twentieth, the city had been the scene of ceremonies to unveil a series of monuments to the leaders in the Confederacy's struggle. Controversy frequently swirled about these occasions. The subjects of the statuary constituted for Southern, and especially Virginia, citizenry a pantheon of heroes to be venerated with an almost religious fervor.

First of the major Confederate memorials was that to Stonewall Jackson, dedicated at Richmond in 1875. This impressive statue was "presented by English gentlemen" who greatly admired "the soldier and patriot" whose deeds it commemorated. Fifteen years would elapse before the impoverished South could manage to provide a similar memorial to Robert E. Lee.

Before the Jackson statue could be unveiled in Richmond's Capitol Square, the ceremony became

Richmond's One-Time Defenders Are Back; And a Gay Lot, These Rebels

At upper left is a group of veterans and guests, while at the right B. F. Red of Little Rock discusses a few campaigns with F. M. Knox of Anson, Texas. In the oval are the Austin twins, J. H. and W. E. Doyle, who rode with Company G of the Seventh South Carolina Cavalry. At the right A. J. Paschal of Austin is seen alighting from a car at Jo Lane Stern Camp. The horse is Old Sorrell, Jackson's mount, and the veterans viewing it are S. Gandy of Austin, R. B. Sitton of Horse Shoe, N. C., F. J. Harlow of Austin, and G. I. Lesesne of Clarendon, S C. At lower left Miss Ina Clendon registers S. T. Powell of Walnutt, Miss.

the subject of acrimonious debate. Negro militia units asked to be allowed to march in the parade, but General Jubal A. Early, the tobacco-chewing, profane president of the Association of the Army of Northern Virginia, strenuously objected. He said he had taken an oath to "support our infernal lying constitution," in order to cast his vote for James L. Kemper as governor of Virginia; and he demanded that Governor Kemper deny the blacks permission to march. If they took part in the parade, fumed Early, it would be "an insult to all Confederates who have any respect for themselves left."

Governor Kemper, who had shown courage previously in his administration when the race issue was concerned, replied that the blacks were going to be in the procession, and "all hell can't change it." He besought Early "for God's sake" not to attend the unveiling. Old Jube disregarded this appeal and came, but for some reason the Negro units did not, although they were expected. Two days earlier they had taken part in a funeral procession for General George E. Pickett. This also had aroused controversy, but owing in part to the intervention of General Joseph E. Johnston, the blacks participated. Perhaps now they failed to show up because they had marched only forty-eight hours before to Pickett's grave in Hollywood Cemetery.

Unveiling of the Lee equestrian statue at Richmond in 1890, on what later became Monument Avenue, was an event to which the South had been looking forward almost since the close of hostilities. Raising the money to pay for it was one problem, and calming the rivalry between two organizations that wanted to take the lead in raising it was another. There were also disagreements concerning the design. The first competition awarded the contract to a "Yankee" sculptor from Ohio. This aroused the Confederate ire of the always bellicose General Early, who wrote Governor Fitzhugh Lee that "if the statue of General Lee is erected after that model," he (Early) would "get together all the surviving members of the Second Corps and blow it up with dynamite." So another competition was held, and the model submitted by Jean Antoine Mercié of France was chosen. This statue, showing Lee seated on Traveller, was received with universal satisfaction. When it arrived from Europe, hundreds of veterans and others turned out and pulled it with ropes to the site at what is today the intersection of Allen and Monument avenues.

Considerable animosity toward the entire concept of a memorial to Lee, however, was expressed in the *Richmond Planet*, owned and edited by John Mitchell, Jr., a Negro councilman. "The men who talk most about the valor of Lee and the blood of the brave Confederate dead are those who never smelt powder" read one of the extremely sour notes appearing in the *Planet*. And on the day of the unveiling, the paper termed the entire proceeding a "legacy of treason and blood" to future generations, and added that "the loyalty so often expressed penetrates no deeper than the surface." One can only admire the reckless courage of a black who would express such sentiments at such a time, when lynchings were taking place frequently in the deep South, and were not unknown in Virginia. If those participating in the unveiling knew of these decidedly heterodox expressions, however, they gave no sign of it.

The unveiling went off without a hitch. There were fifteen thousand Confederate veterans in the parade, fifty generals among them, along with ten thousand other citizens. The procession took two hours and a half to pass. Colonel Archer Anderson was the speaker. He was the son of General Joseph R. Anderson, founder and head of the Tredegar Iron Works; and his address was a eulogy of Lee, combined with a forward-looking approach to the future of the South.

If in the 1890s Lee came under occasional attack from dissenters to the sacredness of the Confederate cause, nowadays his memory is almost universally honored. Even so, there arose occasional detractors.

One of these was Gertrude Stein, the unpredictable lady whose Parisian domicile was the haunt of American writers and artists. She published a book, *Everybody's Autobiography*, in which she delivered herself of the startling pronouncement that Robert E. Lee was "a weak man." This dictum appeared in 1937, and caused a stir at the UDC convention which met at Richmond in that

year. Most of the ladies, however, seemed to have considered the source, for they took the position that Stein was "more to be pitied than censured," as Rhea Talley wrote in the *Times-Dispatch*.

The paragraph from Stein's book, in her characteristically turgid and often baffling prose, follows:

And here I was in Richmond and I had always thought about General Lee and I did think about that. I had always thought., not thought but felt that Lee was a man who knew that the South could not win of course he knew that thing how could a man who was destined by General Scott to succeed him in command of the American armies who knew that war was dependent upon arms and resources and who all that how could he not know that the South could not win and he did know it of that I am completely certain, he did know it, he acted he always acted like a man leading a country in defeat, he always knew it but and this is why I think him a weak man he did not have the courage to say it, if he had had that courage well perhaps there would not just then and not so likely that Civil War but if there had not been would America have been as interesting.

After perusing these words, Mrs. Walter D. Lamar of Macon, Georgia, historian-general of the UDC, pronounced Gertrude Stein "totally ignorant of anything about General Lee or the history of the Confederacy."

Others made such relatively mild comments as "What can this be?" and "Why, I never heard of such a thing." Doubtless they felt that La Stein was talking about something of which she knew little or nothing, so why get excited? She was the author of such works as *Tender Buttons* and *As A Wife Has A Cow A Love Story*, which hardly qualified her to speak authoritatively concerning Marse Robert.

But Mrs. James Lee Tyree of Richmond, who chaired the UDC's music committee, seemed to be as puzzled by some aspects of Lee's career as Gertrude Stein. She came up with the astonishing assertion that Lee, "one of the strongest of men, . . . never surrendered, you know." In support of this amazing thesis, Mrs. Tyree declared that Lee· "said the Confederates would lay down their arms if their implements were returned to them, so they could go back to work."

In contrast to Mrs. Tyree and Mrs. Lamar, the great majority of the UDC delegates seemed content to raise their eyebrows over anyone, such as Stein, who was so benighted as to term Robert E. Lee weak.

Lee's fame as a brilliant general and noble character has recently been subjected to a revisionist interpretation by Thomas L. Connelly entitled *The Marble Man* (1978). Viscount Wolsley of Great Britain said that Lee "was cast in a grander mold and made of different and finer metal than other men"; such New Englanders as Charles Francis Adams and Gamaliel Bradford also were lyrical in praise of this hero of the Confederacy; and Congress made his home, Arlington, a national shrine. Connelly attempts to show that much of this was the result of a concerted effort by a group of conceited Virginians, after Lee's death, to exaggerate his virtues and transform him into a saint.

Advertised as "a shattering new work," Connelly's book doesn't shatter anything of consequence. The knowledge that Lee had a temper, and could not always control it, is nothing new. Connelly also tells us that Lee was seriously discouraged before the Civil War by the slowness of his promotion in the U.S. Army, as though this were highly significant. Many other officers, including George C. Marshall, went through this same experience. The familiar fact that Mrs. Lee was far less interested in social affairs than her husband, and became a semi-invalid, is also hardly a revelation. Connelly speaks very occasionally of what a great man Lee was, and he makes the valid point that Marse Robert was a more complicated individual than some scholars, such as Douglas Southall Freeman, have made him out to be. But in the words of James I. Robertson, Jr., probably the foremost living authority on the Civil War, "To say that this is a bad book is not enough."

Not even the novelist James Branch Cabell, who was no respecter of inflated reputations, found Lee a fit subject for iconoclasm. Cabell's ironic, if not sardonic, approach to ancient as well as contemporary affairs is manifested in the great majority of his observations concerning Lee in *Let Me Lie*. "I cannot avoid remarking the un-Christian and beneficent manner in which

you [Lee] denied to your final years that customary solace of the retired warrior," Cabell wrote, "alike in victory and defeat, of producing his memoirs, in which to expose unflinchingly their writer's grandeur of soul, and to acknowledge with a manly regret the stupidity and the viciousness of his companions and adversaries."

Yet Cabell obviously felt compelled to honor Lee's decision in this regard, and he abandoned temporarily his accustomed irony:

You had reached late middle life. Your health had failed. You were, like all other Virginians then living in Virginia, as poor as that perhaps fabulous fowl to which Virginians refer, without any specified Biblical warrant, "Job's blue turkey hen." The world awaited your memoirs. Many publishers pleaded for your memoirs. You had merely to authorize the appearance of your memoirs in order to ensure your life's future material welfare. You did not even have to be at pains to write your memoirs, for hundreds upon hundreds of your loyal adorers would have performed for you this task-work with delighted gratitude. Your name would sell the results, but you were not willing to sell your name.

In 1907, when the J. E. B. Stuart and Jefferson Davis monuments were dedicated on Richmond's Monument Avenue within a few days of each other, the biggest of all the Confederate reunions took place. The program lasted for an entire week. This was only forty-two years after Appomattox, and the number of surviving veterans who could attend was far greater than was the case for later reunions and dedications. Eighteen thousand veterans came in thirty-one special trains from all corners of the South. Many were still in their sixties, and quite able to march on foot. They could also give an authentic Rebel yell of the sort that had once reverberated on battlefields from Manassas to Chickamauga. These early reunions were accorded enormous prominence in the Richmond newspapers. The entire front page and fifteen or more inside pages were often devoted to Confederate personalities and events.

The Stuart equestrian statue, showing the beau sabreur of the Confederacy astride his high-stepping horse, was the work of Fred Moynihan. After a huge parade it was dedicated with appropriate fanfare on May 30. A vast crowd heard the address of General Thomas S. Garnett, and the statue was unveiled by Virginia Stuart Waller, granddaughter of General Stuart.

Four days later, on June 3, came the dedication of the Jefferson Davis monument. It was designed by William C. Noland and executed by Edward V. Valentine, both of Richmond. More elaborate than the Stuart monument, it included not only a figure of Davis, but a tall pillar, allegorical figures, and rather massive masonry. Another huge parade was followed by more oratory, with General Clement Evans as the principal speaker. The monument was unveiled by Jefferson Davis's only surviving daughter, Margaret Howell Hayes, and her two sons. General Stephen D. Lee, UCV commander-in-chief, pronounced this reunion "beyond doubt the most successful we have had."

Many generals were on hand that year, but a special guest was James A. Jones, Davis's Negro-Indian valet and coachman. Jones was nearby when Davis was captured by Union troops in May, 1865, at Irwinville, Georgia; and he always denied the accusation, circulated in the North, that Davis was wearing feminine apparel and attempting to sneak away. There was little plausibility to this charge; Davis was criticized for many things during his presidency of the Confederacy, but nobody who knew him accused him of lack of courage. The truth seems to be that when Davis saw the Union soldiers approaching in the chilly early morning, he sought to make a getaway, and threw over his shoulders a type of cloak and shawl worn by both sexes. The preposterous lengths to which the Northern press went in misrepresenting this episode were described by Chester D. Bradley in the *Journal of Mississippi History* for August, 1974. Bradley wrote:

The New York *Herald* of May 15 carried a four-column story on page one with sensational headlines, such as, "He Disguises Himself in His Wife's Clothing, and, Like His Accomplice Booth, Takes to the Woods . . . Flourishes a Dagger in the Style of the Assassin of the President." The paper commented, "It is regarded as a fitting termination to such a career as that of the leading actor in the tragedy that he should have been captured while trying to make his escape in his wife's petticoats." The next day (May 16), the same paper published a long disparaging editorial, asserting, "He slipped into his wife's petticoats, crinoline and dress, but in his hurry he forgot to put on her stockings and shoes." On May 27, *Harper's Weekly* published a cartoon

The statue of Stonewall Jackson being unveiled, Capitol
Square, Richmond, 1875.

entitled "Jefferson Davis as an Unprotected Female."
The Confederate President is shown in a hoopskirt
surrounded by jeering Union soldiers. He is wearing a
woman's bonnet, thrown back over his shoulders. On
his right forearm hangs a woman's hatbox. The hoopskirt is elevated in front so that his riding boots are
plainly visible. The following week, June 3, *Harper's
Weekly* published another cartoon. This one was entitled "Ain't You Going to *Recognize* Me?" Davis is
again shown in a hoopskirt. On his head is a woman's
bonnet tied by a ribbon under his chin. Pulling up his
hoopskirt to show the riding boots underneath the
female attire, he is appealing to John Bull and Napoleon
III. John Bull has callously turned his back. Napoleon
III is viewing Davis haughtily through binoculars. In
both of these cartoons a large knife is lying on the ground
at Davis' feet.

Not popular during the war, Davis came to be
widely regarded as a hero and near-martyr after
the close of hostilities when his Union captors put
him in chains at the outset of his confinement at

Fort Monroe and subjected him to other indig-
nities. This treatment provoked so adverse a reaction everywhere, even in the North, that Charles
O'Conor of New York, a leading member of the
American bar, volunteered to defend Davis if and
when he came to trial for treason, and Horace
Greeley, editor of the *New York Tribune*, signed
his bond when he was released on bail. He was
never put on trial.

Even so, long after the war and well into the
twentieth century, there were still Southerners
with no particular admiration for Davis. He had
antagonized a substantial number of people in the
Confederacy with his temperamental behavior,
his irritability, his lack of rapport with some of his
generals, and his apparent belief that he was a
great military strategist. Such antagonism lingered
for generations. As Cabell wrote in *Let Me Lie*
concerning certain Virginians of the period when

he was a child during the 1880s and 90s; "They did not really like this Mr. Jefferson Davis or admire very many of his doings. They stated their reasons in terms which you found to be incomprehensible and of no large interest, because you were wondering why Mr. Davis appeared to be an entirely different person when people talked about him upon platforms."

The emotions stirred by the parades that were a part of every major UCV reunion were admirably described by Henry Sydnor Harrison of Richmond in his best-selling novel *Queed* (1911). Here is one such description, almost certainly of a 1907 grand parade:

From far away floated the strains of "Dixie", crashed out by forty bands. The crowd on the sidewalks stirred; prolonged shouts went up; now all those who were seated on the porch arose at one motion and came forward. . . .

The street had become a tumult, the shouting grew into a roar. Two squares away the head of the parade swept into view, and drew steadily nearer.

At the head of the column came the escort, with the three regimental bands, mounted and bicycle police, city officials, visiting military, sons of veterans, and the militia. . . . Behind the escort rode the honored commander-in-chief of the veterans and staff, the grand marshal and staff, and a detachment of mounted veterans. The general commanding rode a dashing white horse, which he sat superbly, despite his years, and received an ovation all along the line. An even greater ovation went to two festooned carriages which rolled behind the general staff: They contained four black-clad women, no longer young, who bore names that had been dear to the hearts of the Confederacy. After these came the veterans afoot, stepping like youngsters, for that was their pride, in faded equipments which contrasted sharply with the shining trappings of the militia. . . .

Some of the lines were very dragging and straggly; the old feet shuffled and faltered in a way which showed that their march was nearly over. . . . Sadder than the men were the old battle-flags, soiled wisps that the aged hands held aloft with the most solicitous care. . . . Each as it marched by was hailed with a new roar. Of course, there were many tears. There was hardly anybody in all that crowd, over fifty years old, in whom the sight of these fast dwindling ranks did not stir memories of personal bereavement. The old ladies on the porch no longer used their handkerchiefs chiefly for waving.

After the dedication of the Davis and Stuart statues in 1907 there were no more such ceremonies on Monument Avenue until 1919, when on October 11 of that year the equestrian statue of Stonewall Jackson was unveiled at the avenue's intersection with the Boulevard. This monument by F. William Sievers of Richmond showed the redoubtable Stonewall seated on Little Sorrel and facing North; it was said that the Confederate veterans in the nearby Soldiers' Home insisted on his facing that way. Lee's statue was facing South, and they wanted Jackson looking into the eye of the foe. Colonel Robert E. Lee, of Fairfax, Virginia, grandson of the general, was orator on the occasion; and Anne Jackson Preston, Jackson's great granddaughter, did the unveiling. The Virginia Military Institute cadets were the principal feature of the parade, which also included the John Marshall High School cadets of Richmond and various National Guard units.

Last of the statues to be placed on Monument Avenue was that of Commodore Matthew Fontaine Maury, whose torpedo invented in a portable bathtub on East Clay Street, Richmond, was devastatingly effective against Union warships. Maury was known before the war as the Pathfinder of the Seas by virtue of his internationally recognized pioneering explorations of the tides and currents in the ocean, and the wind and weather over it. His statue, dedicated November 11, 1929, is also by F. William Sievers, and it shows him seated, in deep thought, with a globe above and behind him, lapped by stormy waves. It was unveiled at the intersection with Franklin Street by Maury's great grandchildren, Mary Maury Fitzgerald of Richmond, and M. F. Maury Osborne of Norfolk. Governor Harry F. Byrd of Virginia was the speaker.*

The row of five imposing statues of Confederate heroes was now complete, and it made broad Monument Avenue one of the most striking thoroughfares in the United States. John Buchan, the British novelist, following a visit to Richmond, wrote to the Confederate Museum that the city's "memorials of the War Between the States are

* A statue of General A. P. Hill, whose name was on the lips of both Lee and Jackson as they lay dying, was unveiled in 1892 at today's Laburnum Avenue and Hermitage Road. Hill's body was placed beneath it later.

The program of the Sixth Confederate Reunion, 1896, in Richmond invited ex-cavalrymen to become contributing members of the Veteran Cavalry Association, Army of Northern Virginia, in order to raise funds for the statue of General J.E.B. Stuart. The statue was unveiled at the 1907 Reunion.

Courtesy John D. Beall.

conceived with such dignity and simplicity that they are infinitely the most impressive things I saw on the American continent."

The decades that had seen so many reunions and unveilings of statuary in Richmond had been filled with much intersectional rancor, misunderstanding, and controversy, although by 1932 these had pretty well subsided.

The story of North-South relations following the defeat of the Confederacy in 1865 is one of many vicissitudes. Immediately after the surrender at Appomattox there was much bitterness on both sides. Huge casualties had been inflicted on the Confederate and Union forces. The South's agony was redoubled by virtue of the fact that a high proportion of its young men had been killed or maimed for life, much of its territory had been fought over and wrecked, and the entire Southern economy, particularly its agricultural system, almost destroyed. On top of all this, the South had lost the war.

With the exception of General U. S. Grant and a minority of Northerners who shared his generous and large-hearted views, the attitude of the victors, in the years immediately before and just after the end of the war, was hostile and vindictive. This was particularly true of Northern clergymen. For

example, the eminent Dr. Phillips Brooks said when Richmond fell: "We thank thee, O God, for the power of thy right arm which has broken for us the way, and set the banners of our Union in the central city of treason and rebellion." Dr. Henry Ward Beecher declared that the honor of Southerners had a "bastard quality." E. L. Godkin, the famous editor of the *Nation*, pronounced Robert E. Lee, who had accepted the presidency of Washington College, "unfit to train the youth of Virginia." Sidney Andrews, the able correspondent of the *Chicago Tribune*, toured the South and reached the conclusion that Southern civilization was in reality "Southern barbarism."

Yet General Grant wrote: "I am satisfied that the mass of thinking men of the South accept the present situation of affairs in good faith." And Roger A. Pryor, who had been a Confederate general and Southern fire-eater, advised his fellow citizens "to adjust their ideas to the altered state of affairs; to recognize and respect the rights of the colored race; to cultivate relations of confidence and good will toward the people of the North."

It would be folly to suggest, however, that General Pryor's attitude was typical. The Southern people had suffered so much and were in such dire straits that the course he recommended was impossible for most of them. As Paul H. Buck, of Harvard, wrote in his excellent book *The Road to Reunion*, "the South sank to a dead level of unremitting struggle for the necessities of life."

Comments in the Southern press on events during the years immediately after Appomattox were blistering as well as fearless. U.S. District Judge John C. Underwood, a native New Yorker, was presiding in connection with events related to the intended trial of Jefferson Davis. In a charge to the Norfolk grand jury sitting in the case, His Honor said, among other things, that the Confederates had "burned down towns and cities with a barbarity unknown to Christian countries, scattered yellow fever and smallpox among the poor and helpless, and finally struck down one of earth's noblest martyrs to freedom and humanity," namely Lincoln. In reply, the *Petersburg Index* snorted that the judge was an "absurd, blasphemous, devilish, empirical, fanatical, ghoulish, horrible, ignorant, jacobinical . . . Yankeeish zero." Underwood retorted with a blast against the Richmond press, which he held responsible for the "murders, lusts, assassinations, violent and ungoverned passions" of the capital city. The *Richmond Whig* had no intention of taking that lying down. It termed His Honor "an ignorant blockhead" and an "indisputable ass."

The Union general Benjamin F. Butler, familiarly known in the South as Beast Butler, who was reputed, rightly or wrongly, to have purloined silver spoons during his military occupation of New Orleans, came to Richmond in 1868 to harangue the constitutional convention, composed mainly of white carpetbaggers from other states and countries, native scalawags, and blacks. A local newspaper commented on Butler's address as follows:

THE BEAST
Butler spoke, chairman Wardwell smiled, mob applauded, Sublime occasion! Hen-roost and pig-sty thieves forgot their avocation, and chickens and pigs for two hours slept in undisturbed security, while the petty pliers of small trades vied with each other in doing homage to the more successful rascal!

At about this time Innes Randolph composed a bit of verse entitled "The Good Old Rebel," which expressed somewhat humorously the attitude of many Southerners:

Oh, I'm a good old rebel,
Now that's just what I am;
For this "fair land of Freedom"
I do not care a damn.
I'm glad I fit against it—
I only wish we'd won,
And I don't ask no pardon
For anything I've done.

I hates the Constitution,
This Great Republic, too,
I hates the Freedman's Buro,
In uniforms of blue;
I hates the nasty eagle,
With all his braggs and fuss,
The lyin', thievin' Yankees,
I hates 'em wuss and wuss.

I hates the Yankee nation
And everything they do,
I hates the Declaration
Of Independence, too;
I hates the glorious Union—
'Tis dripping with our blood—
I hates their striped banner,
I fit it all I could.

I followed old mas' Robert
For four year, near about,
Got wounded in three places
And starved at Pint Lookout;
I cotch the roomatism
A campin' in the snow,
But I killed a chance o' Yankees,
I'd like to kill some mo'.

Three hundred thousand Yankees
Is stiff in Southern dust;
We GOT three hundred thousand
Before they conquered us;
They died of Southern fever
And Southern steel and shot,
I wish they was three million
Instead of what we got.

I can't take up my musket
And fight 'em now no more,
But I ain't a going to love 'em,
Now that is sarten sure;
And I don't want no pardon
For what I was and am,
I won't be reconstructed
And I don't care a dam.

Like numerous other Virginians, Randolph migrated to Baltimore after the war in search of brighter financial prospects. His song, originally entitled "The Lay of the Last Rebel" and "respectfully dedicated to the Hon. Thad. Stevens," was sung to the tune of the western melody "Joe Bowers."

A graphic example of the South's fight to keep its head above water is seen in the ordeal of young George L. Christian of Richmond, a Confederate soldier whose foot of one leg and the heel of the other were shot off in the furious fusillade at Spotsylvania's Bloody Angle. Christian was out of action, of course, for the remainder of the war. He enrolled in the University of Virginia, which was barely in operation with a handful of professors and a few students who were either under age or severely wounded. Christian and W. C. Holmes of Mississippi, whose right arm had been crippled in the fighting, slept together on the floor of their almost bare room, on one of the blankets they had salvaged from the army, covering themselves with the other. Holmes helped Christian to walk, and Christian helped Holmes with his notes in class. Both finished the course and aided in the rebuilding of the shattered South.

With numerous thousands of young men of the North and the South similarly maimed, and other hundreds of thousands filling graves in Union and Confederate cemeteries, it is hardly surprising that there was bitterness on both sides of Mason and Dixon's Line. *Harper's Weekly*, and its caustic cartoonist, Thomas Nast, never tired of blasting the South for various alleged crimes, such as "forcing Union soldiers to rot in Andersonville and Libby Prisons." As a counterweight to this vituperation there was the *Southern Review*, founded by Albert Taylor Bledsoe in 1867 and edited by him for more than a decade. It spewed hatred against the North and all its works.

Treatment of Northern soldiers in Southern prisons was a perennial subject of denunciatory articles in the Northern press. Yet, although the North had abundant food, medicines, and blankets and the South was sadly lacking in all of them, more Confederate prisoners died in Northern prisons than Federal prisoners died in those of the South. This is shown by official figures released by Secretary of War Edwin Stanton, stating that Confederates who died in Northern prisons numbered 26,436, compared with 22,576 Federals who died in the South. Subsequent totals announced by the U.S. Pension Office were larger in both cases, but the ratio remained about the same, according to Matthew Page Andrews's *Virginia, the Old Dominion*.

The prevailing belligerency in the journals of both sections in the late sixties was mitigated by the appearance, in the *Atlantic Monthly* in 1867, of verses by Francis Miles Finch. Finch had read that women in Mississippi had decorated the graves of Union and Confederate soldiers impartially on Memorial Day. His final stanza follows:

No more shall the war cry sever,
Or the winding rivers be red;
They banish our anger forever
When they laurel the graves of our dead!
Under the sod and the dew,
Waiting the judgment day;
Love and tears for the Blue
Tears and love for the Gray.

This poem's appearance in a magazine not celebrated for its understanding of the South's

CAMP OF FEDERAL PRISONERS ON BELLE ISLE, JAMES RIVER, IN FRONT OF RICHMOND, VA.

—From the 1896 Reunion program. Courtesy John D. Beall.

problems was a refreshing change from the prevailing fulminations against the former Confederacy. It may be assumed, however, that most Northerners were unready for such doctrine. The bloody shirt was being widely and enthusiastically waved.

Some years later, in 1876, James Russell Lowell, the Massachusetts poet whose position had been extremely antislavery and anti-Confederacy, experienced a change of heart. His ode commemorating George Washington's taking command of the Continental Army at Cambridge a century before contained the following lines:

> Virginia gave us this imperial man. . .
> What shall we give her back, but love and praise
> As in the dear old unestranged days
> Before the inevitable wrong began? . . .
> If ever with distempered voice or pen
> We have misdeemed thee, here we take it back.

Memorial Day had been launched at a few places in the South in 1866, and was observed annually thereafter. Graves of Union soldiers were decorated similarly in the North. Majority sentiment there seemed to oppose the placing of flowers on Confederate graves as "honoring disloyalty." During the 1860s and 70s there were uncounted speeches beyond the Potomac and the Ohio denouncing the former Confederacy for its "criminal responsibility," and warning that the victors must not lose the fruits of their conquest. Such vilification was often followed by professions of friendship, but qualified with stipulations that the South would have to confess its guilt in order to receive forgiveness.

A desire to record impartially all facts relating to the war was announced as the objective of the Southern Historical Society, founded at New Orleans in 1896. This society was inspired and supported by the Confederate veterans. General Jubal A. Early was elected its first president, and a more dedicated partisan of the South would have been hard to find. Early's election was not a

happy augury for the authenticity of the society's publications. It continued to function, however, under other auspices, and its first volume of papers appeared in 1876. Additional volumes were issued down the years, until the last of the fifty-two was published in 1959. There is much valuable material here for historians, especially since there is a recently published index.

The death of an old foe of the South, Senator Charles Sumner of Massachusetts. provided the occasion for an important step in restoring friendship between the sections. When Sumner died in 1874, a eulogy for him was delivered in the Senate by Lucius Quintus Cincinnatus Lamar of Mississippi, and this extraordinary oration did much to bind up intersectional wounds. Praising Sumner—a leading abolitionist before the war, and advocate of free Negro suffrage after it—as a man of "high culture," "elegant scholarship," and "strongly marked moral traits," Lamar hailed him as "a great man" and closed with these memorable words: "Would that the spirit of the illustrious dead whom we lament today could speak from the grave to both parties in this deplorable discord, in tones which should reach each and every heart throughout this broad territory: 'My countrymen! Know one another, and you will love one another!'" Many men in the audience were weeping openly when Lamar sat down to tremendous applause. He became a national figure almost overnight.

Lamar's epoch-making address may well have influenced opinion in the North four years later when the lower Mississippi valley was struck by an almost unprecedentedly virulent epidemic of the deadly yellow fever. New Orleans, Memphis, and the Gulf coast were especially hard hit. Northern organizations sent physicians and nurses and various forms of relief. Jefferson Davis wrote that "the noble generosity of the Northern people . . . has been felt with deep gratitude, and has done more for the fraternization of which many idly prate than would many volumes of rhetorical assurance."

President Rutherford B. Hayes contributed to the creation of better feelings between the North and the South when he withdrew the federal garrisons from the former Confederate States soon after his inauguration in 1877. He participated in the Memorial Day ceremonies in Tennessee, where flowers were strewn impartially over Union and Confederate graves; and he made a goodwill tour of the South some months later.

Withdrawal of the Northern garrisons brought Reconstruction to an end. The sufferings of the white South under federal military rule, with carpetbaggers and native scalawags preying on an impoverished and embittered people, were severe. Those sufferings have been exaggerated in some quarters—as, for example, in such books as Claude Bowers's *The Tragic Era*—but they were bad enough. Joel Chandler Harris of Georgia summarized the feelings of the average white Southerner when he wrote: "It was a policy of lawlessness under the forms of law, of disfranchisement, robbery, of repression and fraud. It was a deliberate attempt to humiliate the people who had lost everything by the war, and it aroused passion on both sides that were [sic] unknown when the war was in actual progress." If this sounds extreme, it was how most white Southerners felt at the time; and there was more than a measure of truth in it. Various modern historians—Kenneth M. Stampp, for example—have given a more accurate and balanced view of what happened during Reconstruction.

A favorable omen during the later years of the period was the reversal of attitude by *Harper's Weekly*, which had led the journalistic assault on the postwar South. The paper became much more understanding of Southern problems. The reversal did not extend, however, to Thomas Nast. The vitriolic cartoonist continued, to the best of his ability, to undermine Northern confidence in all things Southern.

In 1881 the centennial of the surrender of Cornwallis at Yorktown in the American Revolution was the occasion for ceremonies participated in by delegates from all sections of the country. Robert C. Winthrop of Massachusetts delivered the oration, in which he "yearned for the restoration of the old relations of amity and good will." James Barron Hope, Virginia's poet laureate for the occasion, expressed similar sentiments in his centennial ode.

National Guard troops from most of the Northern states came to Yorktown for the ceremonies and were heartily welcomed. One

A *Leslie's Weekly* illustration showing President Rutherford
B. Hayes's triumphal visit to Richmond in 1877.

Connecticut regiment even continued on down to Charleston, South Carolina, by ship for several days of intensive hospitality. Its members straggled back northward by train in greatly fatigued circumstances.

Meanwhile Southern writers were contributing articles and stories to Northern journals and were presenting a much different picture of conditions in Dixie before the war from that painted by hostile elements beyond the Potomac and the Ohio. It was too favorable a picture, but it went far to counteract the gross distortions by the abolitionists and their allies. Thomas Nelson Page's novels and stories were useful in correcting false notions, although they were permeated with the fragrance of magnolias and they glossed over the darker aspects of slavery. Page pronounced the antebellum South "for all its faults. . . the purest, sweetest life ever lived," which "made men noble, gentle and brave, and women tender, pure and true." Despite such rhapsodical apostrophes Page showed considerable artistry in his writings, as in the story "Marse Chan." Thomas Wentworth Higginson, an abolitionist who commanded a Negro regiment in the Union Army, is said to have read the story and wept over Page's account of the death of a slaveowner! The writings of Joel Chandler Harris and George W. Bagby also presented a far more favorable picture of life in the Old South than the North had believed existed. All of which had the effect of softening some of the acerbities in intersectional relations.

There were ups and downs in those relations in the 1880s and also, to a lesser extent, in the 1890s. One could never be sure in either decade whether all would be sweetness and light, or whether some individual or organization on one side or the other would erupt with a denunciatory statement or resolution. Memories of the losses sustained in the war sometimes continued to be too vivid for issues to be appraised calmly.

An encouraging event was the amicable reception given in 1885 in Baltimore to R. E. Lee Camp, UCV, by the Society of the Army of the Potomac. Bands played "Dixie," "The Star-Spangled Banner," and "Marching through Georgia" amid applause and cheering. The entire affair was a success. Yet the *Grand Army Sentinel* described Lee the next year as "a breeder of human cattle," while another organ of the Union veterans termed him "a traitor to his flag and country."

The Charleston earthquake of 1886 evoked sincere expressions of sympathy from the North; and Lucius Fairchild, the Grand Army of the Republic's commander-in-chief, hastened to the scene. He requested each GAR camp to collect funds for Charleston's relief, and over $7,000 was raised. The mayor of the city then wired that no further aid was needed. Fairchild wrote later that "the Southern people I meet almost shed tears when they speak of my action in going to Charleston, and I see the Northern papers approve."

But a frightful uproar arose in 1887 when President Grover Cleveland sought to return the captured Confederate battle flags to the South. Any mention of Confederate flags seemed to hit an emotional chord with the Grand Army of the Republic veterans. The organization often objected strenuously to the flying of the Stars and Bars, and when Cleveland said he thought it was time to return the captured banners to the Southern states, there was a terrific hubbub. At a GAR meeting in New York City many veterans had tears in their eyes at the thought of returning the Confederate colors. Commander Fairchild, who had rushed to Charleston's relief, said he had hardly ever in his life been "so wrought up" as he was by this suggestion: "May God palsy the brain that conceived it, and may God palsy the tongue

that dictated it!" This brought wild cheering. GAR posts in many areas joined in protesting, and Fairchild reported that "the 'boys' everywhere nearly overwhelm me with their thanks— they nearly shake my hand off." The son of a Union veteran actually declared that "Cleveland would insult his mother to show his hatred of the Union soldier."

A native of New Jersey who grew up in New York, Cleveland was only trying to promote intersectional amity. He was shocked by the reaction to his proposal, and he withdrew it almost at once. Nothing further was heard of the matter until 1905, when Representative John Lamb of Richmond, a Confederate veteran, introduced a joint resolution in Congress directing the return of the flags by the War Department. By that time the GAR was entirely amenable to the plan, and the resolution went through both the House and Senate without a dissenting vote. In eighteen years there had been a complete reversal of opinion in the ranks of the Northern veterans.

The flags were accordingly returned to the state of Virginia, and entrusted to the care of the Confederate Memorial Literary Society in Richmond. The Grand Camp of UCV in Virginia met in Petersburg that October, and a committee was appointed "to go to Richmond by trolley car and bring over the battered banners." This was done, and the flags were the subject of fervent convention oratory by Governor Andrew J. Montague, former Governor William E. Cameron, and Congressman Lamb.

In the 1930s the flags were transferred to Richmond's Battle Abbey, where they hung for about half a century from the walls located in one wing of the building. By 1982 it became obvious that they were beginning to fall to pieces with age, and the Virginia Historical Society, which then owned Battle Abbey, decided that something should be done to preserve them. Its trustees concluded that since the Confederate Memorial Literary Society, which operates the Museum of the Confederacy, had the facilities to preserve the flags, and the Virginia Historical Society did not have them, the museum would be the proper repository for these priceless relics. Governor Charles S. Robb authorized the transfer by the state, owner of the flags. Since the Confederate

Museum already had a huge collection of flags of the Confederacy, the transfer served to unify the total collection.

Important historical material relating to the conflict of the sixties, prepared insofar as possible in a nonpartisan spirit, was published in 1887. This was *Battles and Leaders of the Civil War*, which had appeared serially during the preceding three years in *Century Magazine*. There were chapters written by many of the principal commanders on both sides, and the whole constituted a major contribution to the literature of the conflict. The publishers solicited material "which eschewed all prejudice and bitterness" and "celebrated the skill and valor of both sides." These objectives were realized to a gratifying degree.

Jefferson Davis, not known previously for his objective approach to the issues of the war and its aftermath, struck a statesmanlike note in the last speech of his life, delivered to a group of young Southern men in 1888, the year before he died: "The past is dead; let it bury its dead. . . . Before you lies the future, a future golden with promise, of expanding national glory, before which all the world shall stand amazed. Let me beseech you to lay aside all rancor, all bitter sectional feeling, and to make your places in the ranks of those who will bring about a consummation devoutly to be wished—a reunited country."

Comment on Davis in the North was usually quite hostile, and when his death occurred, the *Grand Army Sentinel* was true to form. It had the bad taste to observe: "At last Jeff Davis is dead. . . . We are finding no fault with the Lord on that account."

In 1888 the twenty-fifth anniversary of the Battle of Gettysburg was observed with a joint reunion of Northern and Southern veterans who met on the site of the historic encounter. Relatively few Confederates attended; many may have felt that they would not be welcome. But the Union vets met the Confederates in a spirit of cordiality and good fellowship, and the affair went well. The Union general Dan Sickles, who had lost a leg at Gettysburg, struck a conciliatory note when he addressed the group. "Today there are no

victors and no vanquished," he said. "As Americans we may claim a common share . . . in the new America born on the battlefield."

The next step was to arrange for the GAR's national encampment to be held in the South. After futile attempts by Chattanooga, Dallas, and Atlanta to manage this, Louisville finally succeeded. Louisville, of course, is not in Confederate territory, since Kentucky did not secede; but the city is below Mason and Dixon's Line. The official GAR report on the convention declared that "never before have the blue and the gray joined in giving to the world such an exhibition of genuine fraternal feeling and unquestioned loyalty to the Union. . . . The nation's newspapers hailed 'this glorious love feast.'"

During these years the Grand Army was inviting Confederate veterans to join in parades, to attend its meetings, and to share in the erection of monuments. By the early nineties there were more than three hundred GAR posts in the former Confederacy. These posts introduced the color line into their operations, a strangely incongruous attitude for veterans who were supposed to have fought for freedom and the abolition of slavery. The Louisiana delegation to the GAR's national encampment in 1891 stated: "It is right that we should conform to the social laws and rules that surround us." The GAR did elect Charles H. Shute, a Louisiana black, in 1898 junior commander-in-chief as a "gesture of appeasement" to the Negro members.

The so-called Force Bill, introduced in 1890 by Senator Henry Cabot Lodge of Massachusetts, threatened to poison intersectional relations, and, had it passed, would have done so. It was defeated, largely because Northern sentiment for the measure was lukewarm at best. The English historian James Bryce said the bill was "an attempt to overcome nature by law." One apparently well-informed observer declared that when the Republicans failed to pass it, they "tacitly accepted the fact of white supremacy in the South." The measure provided for the appointment of federal supervisors at the polls, representing both major political parties, when as many as five hundred voters asked for this. The bill sought to curb the fraudulent methods used in the South to prevent Negroes from voting. Prevailing sentiment in the

North appeared to accept these frauds. The *Nation*, still edited by E. L. Godkin, urged "patience and sympathy toward the South, whose difficulties have been far greater than those of the North."

Relations between the Northern and Southern veterans appeared to be growing increasingly cordial, and Charles A. Dana, the famous editor of the *New York Sun*, who had served in the U.S. War Department during the Civil War, suggested a joint reunion in New York in 1895. But Ivan Walker, GAR commander-in-chief, vetoed it. Walker said it was "the unalterable conviction of the Grand Army of the Republic" that the North had been right and the South wrong and that "no sentimental nor commercial efforts to efface these radical distinctions should be encouraged by any true patriot."

The *American Tribune*, a paper published by Northern veterans, kept alive the nonsensical charge that during the war the South had sent clothing infected with yellow fever into the North. Not to be outdone, the *Grand Army Record* declared: "It is not true that the leading conspirators who fomented the rebellion thought they were right. They knew they were in the wrong, both legally and morally. But they were recklessly hell-bent on destroying the government of the United States solely and only because Abraham Lincoln . . . had been lawfully elected president."

President William McKinley, a Union veteran, took a different view; and he sought to mend the breach between the sections. In addressing the GAR in 1897 he said: "The army of Grant and the army of Lee are together . . . one now in faith, in hope, in fraternity, in purpose, and in invincible patriotism." The statement was "wildly applauded" by the Union veterans—another example of the ups and downs of intersectional relations during those years.

When the Spanish-American War broke out the next year, McKinley declared that the conflict "has certainly served one very useful purpose in completely obliterating the sectional lines drawn in the last one." While this was an over-optimistic statement, the war with Spain did tend strongly to unite the country. That Fitzhugh Lee and Joe Wheeler, both former Confederate generals,

served in that war was deemed especially gratifying by the GAR. A story, perhaps inevitable, was that in a moment of excitement during one engagement Fighting Joe Wheeler became confused and yelled to his troops: "There go the Blue Bellies! Go get 'em!"

President McKinley suggested that the care of Confederate graves "become a national duty." The United Confederate Veterans debated this at their 1899 convention, and finally concluded that such action would be welcomed, insofar as the graves of Confederates in Northern soil were concerned. They preferred for those in the South to be cared for by Southern women, as in the past.

There was a general awareness in the South that slavery had been a great evil, and that its elimination had been a blessing. It was realized that a civilization based on human servitude, however benevolent, was an anachronism and was unacceptable in the modern age. The general assumption in the South in the early years of this century, when I was growing up, was that if the South had won the war, slavery would have had to be done away with, by one means or another. Rose-tinted descriptions of life in the antebellum era, as encountered in the writings of the Thomas Nelson Page school, were perceived to contain an element of truth, but not the whole truth. The moonlight was not "richer and mellower before the war"; men were not "braver" and women "tenderer" than in later years, as these writers would have it.

A high-school girl in Louisville who refused in 1904 to sing "Marching Through Georgia" became something of a heroine. She was honored for her spunk, especially by the Confederate veterans; but this matter was not regarded as a cosmic issue by most Southerners.

The United Daughters of the Confederacy, always zealous in venerating and upholding the Confederate tradition, held an essay contest in 1908 with "Robert E. Lee: A Present Estimate" as the subject. It was stipulated that students at Teachers College, Columbia University, New York, were to be the sole contestants. The judges were Edwin A. Alderman, president of the University

Veteran Also Can Play Saxophone

of Virginia, and C. Alphonso Smith, dean of the graduate school at the University of North Carolina; and the prize was one hundred dollars. Before the members of the UDC became aware of what was happening, the prize was awarded to a lady from Minnesota whose views were unorthodox, to put it mildly. She said that "Lee was a traitor, in that he sacrificed all to aid the enemies of his country." This Yankee dame also declared that "the South was intellectually dead; most of its people were densely ignorant." The precise reaction of the UDC is lost to history, but it can well be imagined. Judges Alderman and Smith received oral and written shillelaghs from around the map. They defended themselves by saying

that they understood that the UDC had asked for an essay, not a eulogy. That they felt able to award the prize to someone who expressed such opinions was in itself significant. While Southerners generally disagreed strongly with the lady's view, they presumably made allowances for the fact that she was from Minnesota.

The old wounds could still rankle even as late as the 1930s as was reflected in several controversies that arose at the last reunion in 1932. The perennial subject of a joint reunion with the Grand Army of the Republic came up. There were cries of "No! No!"; and the proposal was rejected unanimously. This is difficult to understand, since in previous years such reunions had been held

frequently. From 1881 to 1887, for example, there were "at least twenty-four . . . prominent, formal reunions between the Blue and the Gray," according to Paul H. Buck in *The Road to Reunion*. But, as we have seen, outright hostility was demonstrated by both the UCV and the GAR from time to time, and one could never predict with assurance what the prevailing attitude would be at any given moment.

Often it seemed that the older the surviving veterans were and the farther they got from the war, the more crotchety some of them became, and the more unwilling to let bygones be bygones. General C. A. De Saussure, UCV commander-in-chief, warned the convention of 1932 against textbooks written by authors not in sympathy with the Southern cause, "who inject poison into the minds of children." This may have been a reasonable admonition, in view of the bias in some of the texts emanating from beyond the Mason and Dixon Line. One historical work, David S. Muzzey's *History of the American People*, came under fire from Confederate organizations during the convention, and it was assailed by two historians, although it had been adopted the previous year as a high-school text by the Virginia State Board of Education.

Lyon G. Tyler, former president of the College of William and Mary and a militant defender of all things Southern, assailed Muzzey's work as objectionable because of what Tyler termed its glorification of Abraham Lincoln, and the amount of space devoted to Northern statesmen and soldiers as compared with those of the South. Tyler referred to Lincoln in the course of this controversy as a "boss slacker." I wrote in the *Times-Dispatch* that I saw no useful purpose to be served by the employment of such terminology.

Another historian, Matthew Page Andrews, chairman of the Sons of Confederate Veterans Textbook Committee, leaped into the fray in criticizing Muzzey's work. He said it underplayed the contribution of the Jamestown settlement to the nation's beginnings as well as the contribution of Southern leaders to the founding of the Republic and the framing of the Constitution.

Andrews also deplored that Muzzey could find no "principles" for which the South fought in the Civil War. As a result of these criticisms and the objections of Confederate organizations to Muzzey's book, the author made some modifications, but these were not deemed satisfactory. The book was used in the Virginia high schools until 1938 and then was dropped.

The most vehement of all the controversies during the 1932 convention erupted at sessions of the Confederated Southern Memorial Association, an organization composed of representatives of various women's organizations scattered over the South who were in charge of Confederate cemeteries and similar institutions. A proposed monument at Appomattox was the cause of this unfortunate outburst. The suggestion for such a memorial originated with citizens of Appomattox and the nearby city of Lynchburg, and legislation providing for the shaft had been introduced in Congress by Senator Claude Swanson and Representative Henry St. George Tucker, both of Virginia. The sponsors believed that a suitable marker ought to be placed on the site of one of the country's most historic events. A contest was held for the design, and William C. Noland, one of Virginia's most distinguished architects who had designed the Jefferson Davis Monument in Richmond, was chairman of the committee that made the award. Noland and his associates chose the entry submitted by a Philadelphia firm. It called for a fifty-seven-foot shaft, banded with laurel, with the great seal of the United States on the front, an image of U. S. Grant on one side and of Robert E. Lee on the other, with the pavement at the base of the shaft in blue and gray. The inscription was "North–South; Peace–Unity. Appomattox, the Site of the Termination of the War Between the States, 1861–1865."

It is difficult to see how such a monument could offend any reasonable person, North or South. Yet the CSMA convention went into an uproar over the proposal. A resolution was introduced rejecting the entire concept. The memorial was termed "an insult to General Lee and to every Southern soldier who fought and died for the Confederate cause." An overheated Confederate lady termed it a memorial to "that butcher Grant." It was surmised that General Lee

Scenes and Figures in First Day's Reunion Activities

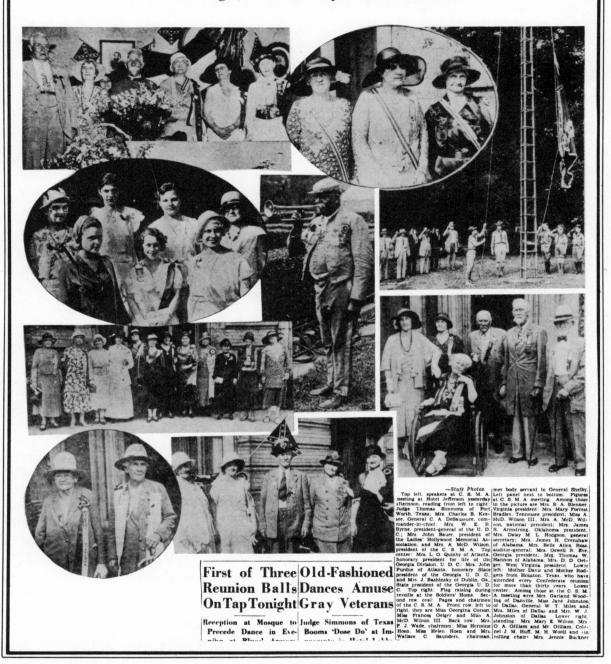

First of Three Reunion Balls On Tap Tonight

Reception at Mosque to Precede Dance in Eve-

Old-Fashioned Dances Amuse Gray Veterans

Judge Simmons of Texas Booms 'Dose Do' at Im-

—Staff Photos.

Top left. speakers at C. S. M. A. meeting at Hotel Jefferson yesterday afternoon. reading from left to right: Judge Thomas Simmons of Fort Worth, Texas; Mrs. Charles B. Kee- see, General C. A. DeSaussure, com- mander-in-chief. Mrs. W. E. R. Byrne, president-general of the U. D. C.; Mrs. John Bauer, president of the Ladies' Hollywood Memorial As- sociation, and Mrs. A. McD. Wilson, president of the C. S. M. A. Top center: Mrs. L. O. Quinby of Atlanta, honorary president for life of the Georgia Division, U. D. C.; Mrs. John Purdue of Atlanta, honorary State president of the Georgia U. D. C. and Mrs. J. Bashinsky of Dublin, Ga., State president of the Georgia U. D. C. Top right: Flag raising during reveille at the Soldiers' Home. Sec- ond row, oval: Pages and chairmen of the C. S. M. A. Front row. left to right. they are Miss Georgina Corson, Miss Frances Geiger and Miss A. McD. Wilson III. Back row: Mrs. P. J. Wade, chairman; Miss Hermine Hoen, Miss Helen Hoen and Mrs. Wallace C. Saunders, chairman.

mer body servant to General Shelby. Left panel next to bottom. Figures at C. S. M. A. meeting. Among those in the picture are Mrs. B. A. Bienner, Virginia president; Mrs. Mary Forrest Bradley, Tennessee president; Miss A. McD. Wilson III, Mrs. A. McD. Wil- son, national president; Mrs. James R. Armstrong. Oklahoma president; Mrs. Daisy M. L. Hodgson, general secretary; Mrs. James H. Crenshaw of Alabama, Mrs. Belle Allen Ross, auditor-general; Mrs. Oswell R. Eve, Georgia president; Mrs. Thomas W. Hannon of Alabama, Mrs. D. D. Gei- ger, West Virginia president. Lower left: Mother Davis and Mother Rod- gers from Houston. Texas, who have attended every Confederate reunion for more than thirty years. Lower center: Among those at the C. S. M. A. meeting were Mrs. Garland Wood- ing of Danville. Miss Jane Johnston of Dallas, General W. T. Miles and Mrs. Miles of Dallas and Mrs. W. J. Johnston of Dallas. Lower right, standing: Mrs. Mary E. Wilson. Mrs. O. A. Gilliam and Mr. Gilliam. Colo- nel J. M. Huff, M. H. Woolf and (in rolling chair) Mrs. Jennie Buckner

—From the Richmond Times-Dispatch.

would never have consented to have his image appear with that of General Grant—a patent absurdity, in view of Lee's admiration for Grant's magnanimity at Appomattox and thereafter.

Mrs. Norma Hardy Britton of Washington, D.C., a member of CSMA, was the sole person to speak on behalf of the monument. She argued that the plan was a "mark of conciliation from the North," a statement which "almost precipitated a fight among the members," according to the *Richmond News Leader*. The great majority took the view that it was a diabolical plot concocted by the North to humiliate the South. When the vote was taken, only four persons supported the plan.

In view of this opposition the congressional sponsors withdrew the legislation, and the whole scheme was abandoned. Restoring the village of Appomattox by the National Park Service to its appearance when the surrender occurred was decided upon instead, and this may well have been preferable on the whole. Yet the reasons for opposing the projected shaft did no credit to those who voiced them. It is gratifying to report that the United Confederate Veterans, also in session in Richmond, did not join with the CSMA in its jeremiads; nor did the Sons of Confederate Veterans, who were likewise in convention there at the time.

A less acrimonious discussion arose during the CSMA conclave when the Augusta, Georgia, Police Band agitated the ladies by appearing to be playing "The Battle Hymn of the Republic," an air not exactly favored in that era in the former Confederacy. All was forgiven, however, when it was pointed out that the band believed it was playing "Glory, Glory to Old Georgia," which had been somewhat unwisely set to the music of the "Battle Hymn."

The bitter controversies of the 1932 reunion were apparently the last of any moment. Fewer and fewer veterans of both armies survived; the issues of the sixties faded farther and farther into the background; and comparable intersectional differences did not arise. There were several mild outbursts in the middle thirties, but after that both North and South began viewing the issues more objectively.

The history of the rise and fall of the veterans' organizations, both Confederate and Union, in the decades between the end of the war and the reunion in Richmond in 1932 is an interesting one. Veterans of both the Confederate and Union forces began forming associations soon after the war. Those formed in the South were not called veterans' associations, since the reorganization of Confederate military units was forbidden. They were often known as "charitable associations," and many were organized by women. Their purpose was to provide relief for destitute veterans or their families, at a time when many were in need; to erect memorials to the fallen; to collect historical data concerning the war; and to promote fraternal relationships.

The Washington Light Infantry Charitable Association of Charleston, South Carolina, was formed in 1865 by survivors of that renowned unit; and the next year the Beauregard Light Infantry Charitable Association made its appearance. The Third North Carolina Infantry Association was organized in 1866, and the Old First Virginia Infantry Association was established in 1867. There were also the brigade associations, such as the First Brigade, South Carolina Regulars, and Terry's Texas Rangers, which tended to be headed by brigadier generals. The oratory which poured forth at these reunions was not only memorable but almost interminable.

The Association of the Army of Northern Virginia was organized in 1870, primarily to erect a memorial to General Robert E. Lee. The Virginia Division of the association was formed in 1871, with General Fitzhugh Lee as president. Powerful and thunderous oratory also marked the subsequent gatherings of this organization. A Louisiana division was established in 1875, and it was active in providing charitable assistance to needy veterans. No other division of the association came into being, although it was hoped to establish one in each of the former Confederate states, all of which had contributed troops to the Army of Northern Virginia.

The charitable and other organizations formed after the war laid the groundwork for founding

Drawing of Soldiers' Home, Richmond, used to raise funds.
Courtesy Richmond Newspapers, Inc.

the United Confederate Veterans at New Orleans in 1889. Intersectional animosities had cooled sufficiently by then for the North to look more tolerantly upon the establishment of a society of former Confederate soldiers and sailors, similar to the Grand Army of the Republic, the organization formed by the Union veterans almost immediately after the war.

General John B. Gordon was elected the first commander-in-chief of the UCV, a post which he was prevailed upon to hold until 1904 despite frequent efforts on his part to give it up. He had made a brilliant record in the Confederate army. Enlisting at age twenty-nine with absolutely no military experience, Gordon became a brigadier

general in less than two years. A born leader of men, fearless and with a commanding presence, he was promoted to lieutenant general before the end of the hostilities. It was his unhappy role to command at the surrender of what was left of the Army of Northern Virginia. Crushed by the realization that they had lost after four years of desperate fighting, the Confederate infantry marched up the hill toward Appomattox Courthouse, with Gordon riding disconsolately in the van.

In command of the Union troops lining the road was General Joshua L. Chamberlain, winner of the Medal of Honor for heroism at Gettysburg. In his book *The Passing of the Armies* (1915),

General Chamberlain described in the following eloquent words his decision to honor the surrendering Confederates:

Before us in proud humiliation stood the embodiment of manhood: men whom neither toils and sufferings, nor the fact of death or disaster, nor hopelessness could bend from their resolve; standing before us now, thin, worn and famished, but erect, and with eyes looking level into ours, waking memories that bound us together as no other bond. . . .

Instruction had been given; and when the head of each division column comes opposite our group, our bugle sounds the signal and instantly our whole line from right to left, regiment by regiment in succession, gives the soldier's salution, from the "order arms" to the old "carry"—the marching salute. Gordon at the head of the column, riding with heavy spirit and downcast face, catches the sound of shifting arms, looks up, and taking the meaning, wheels superbly, making with himself and his horse one uplifted figure, with profound salutation as he drops the point of his sword to the boot toe; then facing to his own command, gives word for his successive brigades to pass us with the same position of the manual—honor answering honor. On our part not a sound of trumpet, nor roll of drum; nor a cheer nor word, nor whisper of vaingon of manor motion of man standing again at the order, but an awed stillness rather, a breath-holding, as if it were the passing of the dead.

Gordon's own wartime reminiscences were remarkable for their complete lack of rancor toward the North, attributable in part, no doubt, to the magnanimity of General Chamberlain at the surrender.

Gordon was involved in Georgia politics for the rest of his life—and in controversies surrounding the railroad industry. There were allegations of improper involvement on his part with the railroads, but the people of Georgia didn't credit the charges. They elected him three times to the United States Senate and once to the governorship. Like the members of the UCV throughout the South, they had confidence in Gordon, and showed it with their votes.

From the end of Reconstruction in 1877 until 1890, Confederate veterans held a majority of the best offices in the Southern states and the Congress. Confederate generals held eighteen of the seats in the 45th Congress, 1877–79, with forty-nine other seats from the South held by lower-ranking Confederate soldiers and sailors. By the 49th Congress, 1885–87, the number of generals had fallen to eleven out of seventy-seven veterans in Congress. Twenty of the remainder had been privates, and from then on men from the lower military ranks far outnumbered the generals and colonels. The last Confederate veteran to serve in Congress was Major Charles M. Stedman of North Carolina, who died in 1930.

Like all veterans' organizations, the UCV was concerned to a greater or lesser degree with obtaining funds from the public treasury for the relief of its members, many of whom were in need. The Grand Army of the Republic was more determined than the UCV to obtain such largesse from the federal government, although as the organization that represented the victorious Union army and navy, its membership was in much less need than were the Southern veterans. The UCV was hopeful that the various states would provide for the destitute former Confederate soldiers and sailors, but as William W. White wrote in *The Confederate Veteran*, "It is surprising that a group of veterans with so much political power asked for so little from their state governments. . . . They viewed themselves not only as veterans but as common citizens and taxpayers."

This is in contrast with the GAR, which exercised pressure over the years for more and more pensions for Union veterans. "The Grand Army kept in view a very tangible purpose, cash benefits for veterans," Dixon Wecter wrote in *When Johnny Comes Marching Home*. "Only in private dared a well-known statesman to say, apropos of a pension bill, that the GAR having saved the country, now wanted it," Wecter declared. Such sentiments seem to have been widely held. The *Nation* spoke for many Eastern liberals when it described the GAR as a political party "formed for the express purpose of getting from the government a definite sum in cash for each member of it." One writer says that "by the nineties . . . anyone who opposed pensions was, at the very least, 'unpatriotic and un-American' and probably a former rebel or Copperhead." A member had warned the organization just before its 1887 encampment against asking for any more pensions, and urged it "to make it clear that the GAR is not organized for the purpose of raiding the U.S.

treasury." This man described the public as sore because of the organization's prehensile propensities. Such propensities are frequently to be found in the ranks of veterans groups—as witness the activities of the American Legion in our own time.

The Republican Party maintained its alliance with the GAR throughout the postbellum era, "a liaison which was about as secret as the relations between Lord Nelson and Lady Hamilton, and just as understandable," Wallace Davies wrote. At its peak in the nineties the GAR had just over 400,000 members. "Vote as you shot!" was its political watchword during the late nineteenth century. It would invite the UCV from time to time to meet with it in joint reunion, but insofar as politics was concerned the organization was anti-Southern and pro-Republican.

The GAR began losing its political potency at the turn of the century. Its members were dying off steadily, and a new generation was taking over. McKinley was the last president who had served in the Civil War. Attrition also was thinning the ranks of the former Confederates. And as the survivors grew much older, they necessarily occupied less influential posts in political and other areas. They contended, as in the past, that "we were overcome by numbers, not whipped, but overcome."

During the leadership of John B. Gordon, from 1889 until 1904, the UCV was at its peak in size and influence. William W. White writes that Gordon's "magnificent, strong voice could reach the largest convention crowd. . . . He carried all with his tact, firmness and common sense. His commanding presence and bearing cast a spell over his fellow veterans." Gordon was succeeded as commander-in-chief in 1904 by General Stephen D. Lee, who served for about four years. Lee was succeeded briefly by General George W. L. Cabell, an effective leader who had commanded the Trans-Mississippi Department from 1894 to 1910. By 1910 the senior Confederate officers were dying off fast, and thereafter no one served as UCV commander-in-chief for more than a few years.

The UCV grew rapidly in the 1890s, and by 1903 there were 1,523 camps, about half of which were in good standing. Active membership stood at around 47,000 veterans, with about 35,000 more who were inactive. Approximately one-third of all living Confederate veterans were in one of these two categories. As time passed and more and more of them died, membership fell swiftly. Fewer than ten percent of the eighteen thousand who attended the great Richmond reunion of 1907, when the statues of J. E. B. Stuart and Jefferson Davis had been unveiled, were able to return to Richmond for the last reunion in 1932. Many had marched in 1907 in the huge parades, but they were unable to march in 1932 and travelled in automobiles. The famous Rebel yell that had echoed from Confederate throats in 1907 was hardly more than a feeble wheeze in 1932.

The Rev. J. William Jones, known as the Fighting Parson for his role in the Civil War (he served in the ranks for a year, and then as a chaplain), was chaplain-general of the UCV for almost nineteen years. The prayer with which he opened the conventions was celebrated: "O God! Our help in ages past, our hope for years to come. God of Israel, God of Abraham, Isaac and Jacob—God of Stonewall Jackson and Robert E. Lee and Jefferson Davis—Lord of Hosts—God of the whole of our common country—God of our Southland—Our God! We bring Thee the adoration of grateful hearts as we gather in our annual reunion today." Such was the prayer for about a decade, and then in 1901 Dr. Jones decided, quite properly, to include "the President of the United States and all in authority under him."

During the Civil War the women of the South made as heroic sacrifices as the men at the front, albeit sacrifices of a different character. After the surrender they were zealous in offering aid to the returned soldiers, in promoting the erection of memorials, and in decorating Confederate graves. Many women's organizations were formed for these purposes in the various Southern communities, and later were attached to the UCV camps as these were established. In 1894, at Nashville, the women's groups were brought together in one organization, the United Daughters of the Confederacy. Since granddaughters of Confederate veterans became eligible for membership, the Real Daughters Club, composed of daughters of

Group of Interesting Sponsors, Maids and Matrons at the Confederate Reunion

Mrs. Anna Pearl Smith

Miss Mary E. Rogers

Miss Margaret Louise O'Brien

Mrs. J. Bryan Peel

Miss Evelyn Castleberry Cook

—From the Richmond News Leader.

veterans, was formed. The UDC has always militantly defended the Southern cause. In fact Wallace Davies writes in *Patriotism on Parade* that "Southern women were notoriously more belligerent than were the old soldiers."

The Sons of Confederate Veterans was organized at the 1896 UCV reunion in Richmond, and has been functioning ever since. In the same year, at Alexandria, Virginia, the Children of the Confederacy came into being. It spread throughout the South, and is still operating, although not so actively as in the past. The organization is composed of grandchildren, great-grandchildren, and great-great-grandchildren of Confederate soldiers and sailors.

A committee was established by the UCV in 1892, with a view to preparing an "impartial history" of the war. It got off to a somewhat shaky start when it recommended that *A Short History of the Confederate States of America* by Jefferson Davis be in every Southern home. Shortly thereafter the Virginia UCV attacked John Fiske's American history, chiefly on the ground that it found objectionable the book's account of South Carolina Congressman Preston Brooks's caning of Senator Sumner of Massachusetts. Brooks was infuriated by the scathing criticism of his elderly uncle, Senator A. P. Butler, that Sumner delivered in 1856 on the floor of the Senate. He accordingly assaulted Sumner while he was seated at his desk, striking him violently and repeatedly with a cane. The cane broke when Sumner was knocked unconscious and seriously injured.

Little or nothing could be said in extenuation of

Brooks's conduct, although he rightly resented the attack on his kinsman. Yet sentiment throughout the South was at such fever heat that Brooks was sent several gold-headed canes by Southern admirers and even one gold-headed cowhide.

The Virginia convention of the UCV refused permission to a representative of Houghton, Mifflin, Fiske's publisher, to address the gathering in defense of Fiske's work. The meeting condemned the historian and praised the writings of Susan P. Lee and the Rev. J. William Jones.

The South's annual Memorial Day in the late nineteenth century attracted large numbers of participants, with at least one prominent speaker on each program. But as the years passed, and the first decade of the new century was reached, interest in the day began to wane. The observance was not abandoned, but participation and interest were less marked.

The Confederate veterans living in soldiers' homes throughout the South were not forgotten, however. As long as they lived, they were objects of attention and solicitude by the Sons of Confederate Veterans and the United Daughters of the Confederacy, especially the latter.

The favorite for many years among all the orators on ceremonial occasions identified with the Confederacy was United States Senator John W. Daniel of Virginia. A Confederate veteran who had been maimed in the war, he was known as "the lame lion of Lynchburg." During a typical speech, lasting for an hour or two, Senator Daniel would be interrupted by great applause after nearly every sentence. As a stem-winder on the platform, in an era when stem-winders were much more numerous than they are today, he surpassed them all.

The UCV continued meeting each year, and the members enjoyed one another's companionship. There were humorous moments, as when Governor James B. Frazier of Tennessee welcomed them to Nashville in 1904: "I welcome you to the grand old hospitable state of Tennessee. I welcome you to the warmth of her sunshine, and if that isn't enough, I welcome you to some of her moon-shine." The governor was followed by the mayor, who announced "the virtual suspension of the law, as far as veterans were concerned." He said his police force had been instructed "to deal gently with those who fall by the wayside under sun or other stroke."

Confederate veterans who attended such gatherings sometimes found the need to take the cure before returning to their abodes. For many months in the *Confederate Veteran* the Nashville Institute announced its Bichloride of Gold Cure for alcoholism and drugs. The institute said it had "a special proposition to make to camps of Confederates." It appears that some of the vets required a week of convalescence before returning from conventions.

Passage of resolutions on many subjects was a favorite exercise at UCV gatherings. In 1912, for example, the organization unanimously condemned "the practice of ladies riding astride at reunions."

A memorable event in the history of the UCV came when the members marched down Pennsylvania Avenue in 1917, after the United States had entered World War I, and were reviewed by President Woodrow Wilson. One banner carried by the old Confederates bore the pungent words *Call on Us if the Boys Can't Do It!* When the Louisiana division hove into view, Chief Justice Edward D. White, a Confederate veteran from that state, left his seat in the reviewing stand and marched past with his comrades.

During the early twentieth century the Confederate mystique was fading throughout the South, but it was still alive. The white-haired veterans in their faded gray coats were to be seen here and there in all eleven states, and they were honored wherever they went. But in the former Confederacy the primary emphasis now was on building up the region and looking to the future. Reunions continued, but with fewer participants each time. By the early 1920s most of the old men who had once worn the gray had passed on, and it seemed clear that the last real reunion would have to be held soon. Richmond, which had been the objective of the Northern armies for four years, was the logical place for it.

Richmond, where the UCV met in 1932, had its beginnings in 1607, when a party of Englishmen came up the James River from Jamestown—site of the original landing ten days before—and planted a wooden cross at the falls. Settlements were established there spasmodically during the next century and a quarter. Meanwhile Indians raided up and down the river, killing hundreds of whites in the great massacres of 1622 and 1644. The first William Byrd, father of the founder of Richmond, settled at the head of navigation on the James in the early 1670s, and was married to the daughter of Colonel Warham Horsmanden, a Royalist officer. Their first child, born in a lonely stone house at the falls, was William Byrd II. But it was not until this Byrd was a grown man, and had spent several years in England and returned to Virginia, that Richmond was founded. In 1733 Byrd, then living at Westover plantation, visited tracts of land that he had acquired along the Roanoke River on both sides of the Virginia–North Carolina line. On his return he recorded these words in his diary: "When we got home we laid the foundation of two large citys. One at Shaccos, to be called Richmond, and the other at the point of Appamattux River, to be called Petersburgh." Major William Mayo, an engineer who was a member of the party, offered to lay out Richmond "without fee or reward." He did not get around to doing it until 1737, at which time Richmond formally came into existence. Prior to that time Byrd had opened warehouses and a store at the falls and had established a ferry. A couple of taverns also were in operation.

Location at the head of navigation augured well for future development, and the little settlement grew gradually. It passed through the Revolution with some serious scars, became the capital of Virginia in 1780, and was incorporated as a city in 1782. In the mid-nineteenth century Richmond was the industrial center of the South. When the Civil War came it was the prime objective of the Union armies.

Richmond in 1932 presented an unusual amalgam—reverence for the Lost Cause combined with a spirit of boosterism. The bitterness occasioned by the death and devastation in the Civil War and the ordeal of Reconstruction had largely vanished, but the city still treasured the memory of Lee, Jackson, Stuart, and Davis. Memorial Day was an important holiday, and it included an impressive parade plus an oration by a prominent speaker. On that occasion, the Confederate graves in Hollywood Cemetery were copiously decorated with flowers and Confederate flags.

While Richmond's reverence for the Lost Cause was less poignant in 1932 than it had been in, say, 1892, it was still vibrant and alive. And it was combined with a newly created spirit of aggressive seeking after prosperity and what was commonly termed Progress. New industries were being brought in; the population was growing; and, almost simultaneously with the great stock-market crash of 1929–30, a skyscraper was erected by a local bank. The then-current joke was that the building was completed just in time for the bank's officers to jump off the top.

I had written an article for the *American Mercury* in 1926, in which I described the spirit of boosterism that had arisen in the city and state. The Virginia State Chamber of Commerce had been established two years previously for the purpose of "selling Virginia to the world." In like manner the Richmond Chamber of Commerce had been transformed from a place in which it was said that "blue-blooded F.F.V.'s often gather to listen to one another's stale talk" into an up-and-coming, live organization. The great harbor of Hampton Roads, it had been said a few years previously, was given to the state by God, and the state was apparently waiting for God to develop it. No longer; development of the port was under way.

It would seem, indeed, that while Richmond and Virginia were engaged in manifestations of progress similar to those beyond the Potomac, the city and the state were trying, at the same time, by means of Confederate reunions and other such events, to maintain their Southern identity. This became increasingly difficult as the pressure of competition with other regions compelled them to seek new industry, to search aggressively for markets for their products, and to expand and

Richmond Salutes Her Defenders

Fred O. Seibel's *Richmond Times-Dispatch* cartoon
welcoming the veterans to the Reunion.

develop otherwise. And as more and more persons from the North and West moved to Richmond, the city became increasingly cosmopolitan and less intensively Southern in its mystique.

In *Richmond After the War: 1865–1890* Michael Chesson reached contrary conclusions concerning the city's business and commercial development. Mr. Chesson has done remarkably fine research on this twenty-five-year period, but in my opinion he has interpreted his data incorrectly. Strangely enough he relies heavily on the caustic observations of Henry James, the New York-born novelist who spent much of his life in England and who visited Richmond for a few days in 1905 (not 1903, as stated by Chesson).

In *The American Scene* James has a chapter on that visit to Richmond. He says he expected to be favorably impressed by the city but was not. Almost everything that he saw during his all-too-brief sojourn was not to his liking. Chesson gives great weight to impressions gained by this visitor as he moved casually about, looking in at the Confederate Museum, the Capitol, and a few other places, and inspecting the equestrian statue of Lee. Chesson actually devotes most of his epilogue to scathing quotations from James, who is highly critical of the South's role in the Civil War. James's thinking concerning that role, which he terms "the very heaven of futility" and "pathetic in its folly," dominates his attitude toward Richmond in 1905. Chesson sums up:

Richmond inherited the worst of both the Old and the New South. The racism and conservatism of life before the war became even more embedded in its society, but much of the antebellum graciousness, noblesse oblige, and disdain for money was gone, replaced by a materialism and a superficiality vividly perceived by Ellen Glasgow. The rights of workers, women and blacks were little more respected, and the need for a good public school system, for libraries, and for other progressive features of modern urban life were scarcely more recognized in 1890 than in 1860. The tragedy of Richmond after the war was that the white leaders, after two decades of flirtation with progress, returned to a cause that they had all but abandoned and embraced the dead thing with a passion they had never felt while it lived.

Evidence in the book for these assertions is scanty. Indeed, a good many of Chesson's own facts and statements contradict these allegations.

By 1890, he says, "a passion for the Lost Cause became the vogue for white residents." The evidence for this charge seems to derive from the prejudiced appraisals of Henry James, together with the not exactly damning fact that several statues of Confederate heroes were erected in Richmond, beginning in 1890. Nor do I find anything in Chesson's book to buttress the assertion that "much of the antebellum graciousness, noblesse oblige and disdain for money was gone." As for his claim that Richmond was racist, I venture to suggest that it was less racist than the great majority of Southern cities. If his charge is valid, how does he explain the statement in *The Negro in Virginia*, published in 1940 under the sponsorship of Hampton Institute, that "from 1890 to 1920 . . . Richmond was considered the most important center of Negro business activity in the world"? Admittedly Richmond was extremely backward in obtaining a public library; but the assertion that "the need for a good public school system" was "scarcely more recognized in 1890 than in 1860" is absurd.

Chesson's declaration that "after two decades of flirtation with progress" the city's white leaders "returned to a cause that they had all but abandoned"—namely the Lost Cause—scarcely explains the progress that more than quadrupled the population between 1860 and 1920 and gained the Federal Reserve Bank for Richmond in 1914 after Richmond competed with much larger Baltimore. Nor does it explain the presence in the city in the early 1920s of "the largest cigarette factory, woodworking plant, mica mills, baking powder factory and plant for reproducing antique furniture" on the globe.

Louis D. Rubin, Jr., elucidates Richmond's obeisance to the Lost Cause by arguing directly contrary to the thesis of Chesson. In *Virginia: A Bicentennial History* Rubin says: "It was perhaps because of the . . . swiftness with which the city recovered commercially and physically from the devastation of the war that Richmond surpassed all others in the state and even in the entire South in the public devotion that it paid to the Confederate past." In other words, the city's strong emphasis on its wartime heritage was not owing merely to its having been the wartime capital but also to the fact that this was a way of self-

consciously asserting its old Southern identity, when actually it had become a border-state city, a commercially oriented, middle-class American city doing its best to better its lot and live in the present.

There were numerous shrines and monuments in Richmond relating to the Confederacy which would be of special interest to the delegates who were coming to the last reunion of the United Confederate Veterans in June, 1932. Among these were the Museum of the Confederacy, formerly the Confederate White House; Battle Abbey, the memorial to the men and women of the South to which citizens from all over the region contributed, famous for its Civil War battle flags and its fine wartime murals by Hoffbauer; St Paul's Episcopal Church, where Lee worshipped and where President Jefferson Davis was attending the Sunday service on April 2, 1865, when word came to him from Lee that Petersburg could not be held and that Richmond would have to be evacuated at once; the Valentine Museum, with the death mask of Jackson, and the plaster model for Edward V. Valentine's recumbent statue of Lee at Lexington; the Virginia Historical Society, located in Lee's wartime residence, with objects and manuscripts relating to the war; the mounted remains of Little Sorrel, Jackson's favorite war-horse, on view at the Soldiers' Home, where the steed had died in 1886; the Capitol, where the Confederate Congress met during the war, and where in April, 1861, Lee had received his sword as commander of the Virginia forces; Hollywood Cemetery, with its graves of thousands of Confederate soldiers, and broad Monument Avenue, with its statues of Lee, Jackson, Stuart, Davis, and Maury.

Richmond had many other significant historical attractions. These included old St. John's Church, where Patrick Henry electrified the revolutionary convention of 1775 with his impassioned call for liberty or death; the house where John Marshall, our greatest chief justice, lived for nearly half a century; the Edgar Allan Poe Shrine in the Old Stone House, the city's oldest surviving residence, and the adjacent museum, with important relics

of the internationally renowned poet; Monumental Episcopal Church, opened in 1814 on the site of the terrible theater-fire of 1811, in which Governor George W. Smith and seventy-one others perished; and the Capitol, designed by Thomas Jefferson, with Houdon's statue of Washington in the Rotunda, a building that has been the scene of many historic events in addition to those already mentioned, including the trial of Aaron Burr for treason in 1807 with John Marshall on the bench and John Randolph of Roanoke as foreman of the grand jury.

In 1932 Richmond was preparing in all possible ways for the coming of the Confederate veterans. Douglas Southall Freeman, editor of the *Richmond News Leader*, already recognized as a leading authority on the Civil War although his masterly books on the subject lay in the future, hailed the approaching gathering. Under the caption *They Are Coming Again!* he editorialized: "Nothing like next week's reunion has ever been held in America. Nothing like it can ever be held again."

The convention's general chairman was Robert T. Barton, Jr., a prominent young lawyer whose family had a stunning record in the Civil War. His father fought in the famous Stonewall Brigade, and three of his uncles were killed in the war. Another uncle, Major Randolph Barton, was wounded five times and had seven horses shot from under him. He lived to become a leading attorney in Baltimore. Robert Barton, Jr., a captain of field artillery in World War I, would serve as a colonel in World War II. His assistant chairmen were G. Jeter Jones, Henry S. Hotchkiss, and Lee O. Miller.

It was taken for granted that there would be ailing veterans at the conclave, and instructions for their care were issued by Dr. Robert C. Bryan, chairman of the medical committee. He pointed out that men averaging in age from 85 to 90 "require the greatest care and attention," and urged that, in the event of any accident or illness, Memorial Hospital be called for an ambulance. The public was also asked to invite into their homes any veteran who needed to lie down or who wanted a drink of water or anything else.

"Please remember," Dr. Bryan went on, "that

Albert Everett, 104 years, Murfreesboro, Tenn., who served as General Lee's cook for practically the entire war period. He is a frequent attendant at reunions.

"Uncle" Stever Everhart, 104 years of age, of Rome, Ga., who is a familiar figure at all Confederate reunions. He declares that his Georgia mistress sent him to war to look out for her son, his young master, and he thinks he made a good job of the task. His principal job, he says, was to get all the chickens used in the army, and he doesn't recall ever failing to deliver the goods as needed. He has posed twice for the movies. He is worried at the present time over the loss of his suitcase.

—From the Richmond Times-Dispatch.

these old men know much better than you what they have been accustomed to eat, and the routine of their lives. Let them have what they want. Eighty-five years of habit cannot be changed in twenty-four hours." Addressing the housewives of Richmond, Dr. Bryan opined: "You are probably a good housekeeper and excellent hostess, but you are not a doctor. . . . You must remember that the heat, advanced age, excitement of travel, irregular habits, and the reunion work a great hardship on these frail bodies."

The Soldiers' Home hospital was upgraded for the occasion, with medical men in charge during the day and trained nurses on duty. There appears to have been no abnormal number of serious illnesses in the ranks of the vets, and only the usual minor afflictions.

Delegates to the reunion were greeted on the opening day by a poem on the front page of the *Richmond Times-Dispatch*. Entitled "To the Lacedemonians," it had been commissioned by the newspaper and had been written by the distinguished poet Allen Tate. The poem is preceded by the words "*The Old Confederate on the Night before the Reunion Speaks partly to Himself, partly to Imaginary Comrades.*" It opened with these lines:

> People, people of my own kind—today
> Home-folks, but strange with a new light
> In the face; and the streets hard with motion
> And the hard eyes that look one way.
> I am here with a secret in the night;
> I am here because the dead wear gray.
>
> It is a privilege to be dead. You
> Cannot know what absence is, nor what
> The odor of pure distance is, until
> From you—slowly dying in the head—
> All sights and sounds of the moment, all
> The life of sweet intimacy shall fall
> Like a swift at dusk, and the heart of time,
> The lightning pulse is bled. . . .

The poem ended:

> Soldiers march! We shall not fight again
> The Yankees with our guns well-aimed and rammed,
> For all are Yankees of the race of men
> And this too, now, the country of the damned.
>
> Poor bodies crowding round us, white of face,

> Eyeless with eyesight only, bones of power;
> Stricken sublimities of time and space—
> They are the fragments of an ancient tower
>
> That stood with easy strength upon the land
> Pouring its long white ray into the mind—
> Damned souls, running the way of sand,
> Into the destination of the wind!

Behind this poem lay Allen Tate's deep dedication to the philosophy of the Nashville Agrarians expressed in their symposium *I'll Take My Stand*. Tate was saying that the South fought the war to preserve its way of life, a leisurely life on the land, with a sense of values that conflicted drastically with that of the urban materialistic North. But once the war was over, the South began aping the Yankees by building a civilization similar to theirs. This could only mean, in his view, that it was a "privilege to be dead," rather than to follow the sordid money-grubbing road laid out by the North. The Southern survivors of the conflict of the sixties are "damned souls," Tate says, since all Southerners have now become Yankees in spirit.

The poem's title, "To the Lacedemonians," refers to the Spartans who died at Thermopylae. The Confederates who fought and died for the standards and values that they treasured are compared to the heroic Spartans who gave their lives in fighting the Persian invaders.

One may assume that the poem, for all its merits, was not understood or appreciated by the great majority of the Confederate veterans as they arrived in Richmond. Only persons who were aware that it reflected the philosophy of the Nashville Agrarians could fully understand it. And the line "slowly dying in the head" must have been regarded by many as something less than appropriate to the occasion. Tate was apparently referring to the blurring of memory that comes with age, as contrasted with the emotion of the heart, which remains as fierce and loyal as ever.

The special events in Richmond began on Monday, June 20, when General C. A. De Saussure of Nashville, commander-in-chief of the United Confederate Veterans, arrived with his entourage to a salute of seventeen guns. The Richmond

Light Infantry Blues was his local escort. This salute was followed by the raising of the Confederate flag over the Capitol. Several bands gave a concert that evening at Camp De Saussure, the special designation given Lee Camp Soldiers' Home in Richmond's West End, where many of the visiting veterans were quartered.

Lee Camp No. 1, UCV, had been organized in 1883 at Richmond to care for needy veterans. A site for a Soldiers' Home at the intersection of Grove Road, later known as Grove Avenue, and what was later termed the Boulevard was acquired the next year. The home opened January 1, 1885. As a starter an old building was renovated, and other structures were acquired gradually. When completed the home included cottages, a dining hall, a hospital, and a chapel. Cottages were donated by various individuals; the state of Virginia appropriated $35,000; and the city of Richmond raised $5,000 for the chapel. From the chapel, a modest frame structure still standing in 1983, some seventeen hundred veterans were buried. All but two of the buildings were torn down after the last inmate died in 1941. The Virginia Museum of Fine Arts occupies the site. The Richmond home, one of fifteen scattered over the South, was the best known.

The GAR post in Newark, New Jersey, was the first of all the contributors to the home; it sent one hundred dollars in gold in the early 1880s. Shortly thereafter General U. S. Grant sent his check for five hundred dollars. He was invited in 1884 to attend a fair to raise money for the institution but found it impossible. The former commander of the armies of the Union wrote, wishing success to the committee in charge in its effort to erect "for all the brave men who need it a home and rest from cares." And he went on to say: "The men who faced each other in deadly combat can well afford to be the best of friends now, and only strive for rivalry in seeing which can be the best citizens of the grandest country on earth."

When General Grant died in 1885, both Richmond and Virginia showed their admiration for the man who had demonstrated such magnanimity. Governor William E. Cameron and four companies of Virginia militia attended the obsequies in New York, while the Virginia State Democratic Convention passed resolutions of sorrow. In Richmond business was suspended throughout the day of the funeral, and flags were flown at half-mast. The Richmond Howitzers fired a salute.

In 1932 many of the veterans had stopped over in Petersburg en route to Richmond to witness the dedication of the Petersburg National Military Park. The program included a pageant with seven scenes, among them the Battle of the Crater and the battle of June 9, 1864, when the city was saved from a surprise attack by the bravery of a citizen force. This latter feat is commemorated on a tablet in historic Blandford Church, which tells of "the Citizen Soldiers of Petersburg, the gray-haired sires and beardless youth who . . . laid down their lives near this venerable church in successful defense of our altars and firesides."

Richmond opened its heart to the men who had fought for the South from 1861 to 1865. "Everything is Free," the convention program proclaimed, and the city's ordinary citizens, as well as its leaders, put forth all possible efforts to make the visitors welcome and at home. They in turn gave many evidences that they were enjoying themselves.

This reunion was not an occasion for stirring up intersectional animosities and opening old wounds. Although there were instances when lingering antagonism against the North was shown on specific issues by aged individuals, for the most part it was a good-natured gathering held in a relaxed atmosphere. Hospitality was lavish and virtually unlimited, although this was the bottom of the Great Depression.

Striking evidence of intersectional amity was seen in the presence of two especially honored guests. They were Dr. George Bolling Lee, the only surviving grandson of General R. E. Lee, and Lieutenant Colonel Ulysses S. Grant III, grandson of General U. S. Grant. Dr. Lee and Colonel Grant got along famously and were photographed shaking hands most cordially.

Confederate flags lined Broad Street, decorated the statues of Confederate heroes, and hung from homes. The flag of the Confederacy flew from the Capitol throughout the convention, but it was not

the same banner that fluttered there when Richmond fell on April 3, 1865. That flag, hauled down and carried off by a Union officer, was graciously returned in 1927; but it was too fragile to be flown during the reunion. It had been made while the Civil War was in progress, at the request of Virginia's Governor "Extra Billy" Smith, who asked the Misses Sallie and Margaret Munford to fashion a new flag to replace the tattered Confederate oriflamme atop the Capitol. They did so, and by a remarkable set of circumstances Miss Sallie Munford was present more than six decades later at the ceremony in Richmond for the flag's return. She was then Mrs. Charles H. Talbott, and she readily identified the flag as the one that she and her sister had stitched in their Franklin Street home at the height of the Civil War.

Veterans attending the 1932 reunion were among the visitors to Capitol Square, where the Confederate banner flew. I saw them sitting on the benches feeding peanuts to the squirrels. The peaceful scene was in glaring contrast to that of April 3, 1865, when after the few remaining Confederate forces had left the city, the area immediately south of the Square became a roaring inferno, and the Square itself was filled with terrified women and children. The fire had been set in tobacco warehouses by Confederate officials, in an effort to prevent the tobacco from falling into Union hands, but a high wind sprang up and spread the flames. Every effort was made by the Union troops to control the conflagration when they took over the city, but Richmond's business district was virtually wiped out.

At 6 P.M. each day a sunset gun was fired from Capitol Hill and at 8 P.M. there was special entertainment at Camp De Saussure. It included musical numbers, dancing of the minuet and Virginia Reel by local high-school pupils, Old Time Fiddlers, the Sabbath Glee Club of Negro singers, Blackface Artists, a number called "Hack and Sack," and other skits. A similar program was offered on the next two nights.

Before these programs began, space was left in the schedule of events for "Amos 'n' Andy," the radio program that achieved almost unprecedented

popularity and ran uninterruptedly for thirty-two years. "Amos 'n' Andy" was such a universal favorite that it was listed specifically for 6 P.M. daily on the UCV's convention program, so that no competing event would interfere with the veterans' slapping their knees and guffawing at the humorous sallies—along with some forty million other Americans. Many of the delegates would undoubtedly have felt deprived if this opportunity had not been offered. Motion-picture houses in that era actually interrupted their programs and piped in the complete dialogue of "Amos 'n' Andy" for fifteen minutes, after which the showing of the film resumed. The two principal characters were played by Freeman Gosden and Charles Correll, white men who impersonated blacks. Other "blacks" were Kingfish, Lightnin', Madame Queen, and Brother Crawford. For decades their antics were regarded as inoffensive, but as the civil rights movement gathered momentum in the 1950s they came to be considered objectionable, and the show finally went off the air. The old vets relished it immensely in 1932.

On the opening day of the convention I was sent out to the Old Soldiers' Home by the *Times-Dispatch* to report on the state of affairs among the newly arrived delegates. They were getting acquainted, and swapping stories of the war, some of which were of decidedly dubious authenticity. The federal government had furnished, without charge, enough army cots to care for two thousand men, together with sheets, blankets, pillows, and pillowcases. About 750 visiting veterans were staying at Camp De Saussure, with some 650 more at Camp Robert E. Lee in Robert E. Lee School, and 100 at Camp Father Ryan in Benedictine School.

"There was nothing of rancor in their good-natured reminiscences," I wrote. "Gone was the ancient animosity for the 'Yanks.' They talked of the war as though all the delirium of the sixties had been obliterated by the flood of years. . . .

"They sat under the trees or on the cottage porches, talking of the days of long ago, when 'Marse Robert' led them to victory, and the shell-torn banners of the Confederacy perched for one

triumphant moment on the heights of Seminary Ridge, only to be withdrawn when reinforcements failed to come up."

Unfortunately I had the shell-torn banners of the Confederacy perching at the wrong place at Gettysburg. It was Cemetery, not Seminary, Ridge which marked the high tide of Pickett's immortal charge. Seminary Ridge was the height from which Lee surveyed the sanguinary scene.

The benches under the trees at the Soldiers' Home were an admirable locale for the recounting of one's heroic exploits during the war or deeds of derring-do attributable to others. A typical stretcher was the yarn related by one hardened warrior, reputedly from the state of South Carolina. "When we was blowed up at the Crater," said he, "me and my men was th'owed up in the air. As we went up, we met our captain a-comin' down, and as he went by he hollered, 'Rally boys when you hit the ground!'"

Breakfast was served for the visiting delegates at Camp De Saussure from 6 A.M. to 9 A.M. Apparently it was theorized that at least a few of the old boys were accustomed to rising early and breakfasting betimes. For those of a somewhat more somnolent disposition there was reveille at 7 A.M. to the rousing notes of one of several bands.

The musical organizations that played for these and other functions during the convention were the Mississippi State Teachers' College Band; the Augusta, Georgia, Police Band; the Little Rock, Arkansas, High School Band; the Charlottesville, Virginia, Municipal Band; and the Clarksville, Virginia, Boys' and Girls' Band.

At least once a day, and usually twice, there was an illustrated lecture in the Soldiers' Home Chapel on Generals Robert E. Lee and Stonewall Jackson, "courtesy of Mrs. Lottie K. Browne."

All the Richmond hotels were jammed with visitors—not only members of the UCV but also those of the Sons of Confederate Veterans and the Confederated Southern Memorial Association, which were holding conventions in the city. Many were guests in private homes. Others were in various lodgings arranged in schools and colleges.

The prohibition law was still in full force in Richmond and everywhere else in 1932. Repeal did not come until the next year. Although there was no open violation of the law during the convention, insofar as I was aware, it may be safely assumed that prohibition was no more effective at that time than at any other. Hospitality around the flowing bowl was entirely unofficial, but in private homes and elsewhere one may take it for

granted that successful efforts were made to assuage the thirst of the visitors. The two Richmond newspapers, the *Times-Dispatch* and *News Leader*, were both vigorously opposed to the dry law as being completely unenforceable and objectionable on other grounds as well. They recorded the confiscation and destruction on the city dump of liquor seized during the convention. Whether this raid had any relation to the presence of the Confederates was not made known. Another amusing episode occurred when nine bottles of confiscated home brew blew up in police court, furnishing an obligato to the music of the convention bands outside.

The local papers gave lavish coverage to the convention, with hundreds of pictures and many columns of type, although they by no means matched the amount of space devoted to the reunions of 1890 and 1907. Much space also was devoted to the Democratic national convention, which was meeting in Chicago to nominate a candidate for president of the United States. Franklin D. Roosevelt was making his successful bid for the nomination, and there was a short-lived presidential boom for ex-Governor Harry F. Byrd of Virginia.

During the UCV convention the Richmond newspapers adopted the practice of identifying each of its writers by a forebear who served in the Confederate forces. My contributions were accordingly signed "By Virginius Dabney, grandson of Captain Virginius Dabney, CSA, of General John B. Gordon's staff."

After my initial trip I went out to the Old Soldiers' Home again, in order to interview one or more of the half-dozen Negro body servants who were attending the convention. There I found Uncle Bill Wilson, who boasted of his prowess in purloining chickens, pigs, corn, and watermelons for his master. On one of these foraging expeditions he encountered a Yankee bushwhacker, who fired on him. Uncle Bill's horse bolted and slammed into a tree, banging up Bill's knee so badly that he had been a cripple ever since—for some seventy years. "Yas, suh, I'se crippled," he said sadly,

"and I reckon I always will be"—an assumption that appeared hardly susceptible of contradiction.

But the most celebrated of the black servants was undoubtedly Uncle Steve Eberhardt, whose prowess as a raider of hen roosts was proverbial. He attended all UCV reunions over many years, with chicken feathers protruding from his hat and clothing. Captain James Dinkins wrote in the *Confederate Veteran* of his appearance and actions in Richmond. Uncle Steve was invited to the platform at the Mosque, where the convention sessions were being held, Dinkins said. He was a member of the 10th Georgia, and he wanted to speak. "His hat and his pockets were full of chicken feathers," Dinkins wrote. Steve stated: "I am a hundred and seven years old, I have always been a white man's nigger, and the Yankees can't change me, suh!" He drew loud applause.

Obviously a relic of a bygone era, Uncle Steve appears in Bell I. Wiley's *Southern Negroes: 1861–1865.* Wiley wrote that "the bosom of his 'Confederate Gray' overcoat was almost completely covered with reunion badges." Flaunting the tailfeathers of his pilfered fowls, the aged black proclaimed himself "the biggest chicken-thief in the Confederacy."

These Negro body servants sat under the trees at the Soldiers' Home with the white veterans. Many of both groups were smoking their pipes or chewing their plugs. There were emotional moments, as when one of the white Confederates was asked which general he served under in the war. "Jackson, sir," came the proud reply, as tears welled in the old man's eyes.

Captain Dinkins wrote that the convention was attended mainly by "generals," and that no more than fifty nongenerals were on hand for any of the official sessions. He himself appeared on the program as Major General Dinkins. "There were a great many generals," said he. "I doubt if Caesar had as many generals in his big army when he crossed the Rubicon as there were in Richmond." These UCV generals had been officers of lower rank, even privates, during the war; the actual generals were all dead. On the evening program Wednesday, June 22, there were no fewer than twelve generals either making speeches or introducing speakers. The convention was called to

General Homer Atkinson, on the left, new commander-in-chief of the Confederate Veterans, and General C. A. DeSaussure, retiring commander-in-chief, on the right, as they rode along in the commander's car in the reunion parade, which was the closing feature of the forty-second gathering of these heroic sons of the South since the war.

order by General William McK. Evans, commander of the Virginia Division, UCV. He presented General W. B. Freeman, honorary commander for life, and father of Douglas Freeman. Another notable participant in the program was the Rev. Giles B. Cooke, honorary chaplain-general for life and the last surviving member of General Robert E. Lee's staff.

A significant relic on view during the conclave was the tremendous sword of Heros von Borcke, the Prussian dragoon who crossed the Atlantic and ran the blockade to fight for the Confederacy. Von Borcke, who became General J. E. B. Stuart's adjutant-general, had knelt by Stuart's bed, his huge frame wracked with sobs, as the great cavalryman's life ebbed away following his mortal wound at Yellow Tavern.

Also to be seen during the convention was "an original John Brown pike," wielded by Brown or one of his men in their attempt at Harper's Ferry to incite a slave insurrection on the eve of the war, an ill-starred effort that ended, for Brown, on the gallows. But while the fanatic Brown forfeited his life, his soul "went marching on." Stephen Vincent Benét, in his memorable poem *John Brown's Body*, speaks of Brown's "singing bones" and the inspiration they gave to the antislavery forces of the North. "The Battle Hymn of the Republic" and the song "John Brown's Body" were sung by the Union Army's marching thousands; and the war became, in the minds of many, a great antislavery crusade. Brown himself wrote that he was "worth inconceivably more to *hang* than for any other purpose."

Senator Tom Connally of Texas spoke in stentorian tones at the opening of the Sons of Confederate Veterans convention in the Mosque. Scorning the microphone, considered absolutely essential by virtually all speakers in the huge hall, the orator from the Lone Star State shook the rafters as he addressed a packed house.

"I do not like the words 'Lost Cause,'" the speaker boomed. "The example set by Southern women during the war can never be called lost. Nor is Jackson's military skill lost to military students, nor the towering military leadership of Lee." Connally decried the statements of some critics that the South fought "to keep the slaves," saying that the vast majority of the men who

fought never owned a slave and never expected to own one.

Senator Connally also spoke at the dedication of the handsome new building of the Home for Confederate Women, adjoining the Old Soldiers' Home. The widows of Confederate soldiers had been housed for many years in an extremely modest house on Grace Street. Most of them had died by 1932, when the well-appointed new residence was opened. Now, as the number of widows dwindled, daughters of the men who fought for the Confederacy were placed in the institution. A half-century later, in 1983, there were no widows and thirty daughters in a building that accommodates seventy-nine.

Dedication of the Richmond Battlefield Parks, comprising the blood-soaked fields around the city over which the Confederate and Union armies fought, was a feature of the reunion program. Five hundred acres were included in the total parks area, and the ceremony was held in a grove at Frayser's Farm, scene of one of the desperate encounters of the Seven Days. Battlefields included in the park system, which was ceded to the state, were those of Seven Pines, Mechanicsville, Gaines' Mill, Savage Station, Frayser's Farm, Malvern Hill, Bethesda Church, Cold Harbor, and Fort Harrison.

Douglas Southall Freeman and J. Ambler Johnston, a prominent Richmond engineer, were primarily responsible for the creation of this park system. Johnston, like Freeman, was a great authority on these battlefields. He arranged the program of dedication, and Freeman took part in it. Tazewell M. Carrington, president of the Richmond Battlefield Parks Corporation, presided and formally presented the park area to the commonwealth. Lieutenant Governor James H. Price accepted it. Governor John Garland Pollard appeared on several other programs during the convention but not this one.

Major General Lytle Brown, chief of engineers, U.S. Army, was the principal speaker. The affair took an unexpected turn when Douglas Freeman sought to introduce him. The Confederate veterans in the audience decided that they wanted to get

This photograph gives some idea of how the veterans crowded forward to shake the hands of Colonel U. S. Grant, III, grandson of General U. S. Grant, who was accorded an ovation when he was presented to the gathering at the battlefield park dedication. His appearance, with Dr. George Bolling Lee, grandson of General Robert E. Lee, was one of the thrilling incidents of reunion week.

—From the Richmond News Leader.

into the act. As Freeman began discussing some of the events that had occurred on this historic ground, veterans began interrupting with a wide-ranging list of questions. "The veterans insisted that he go on and name all Confederate officers through the rank of colonel, all brigades, all divisions and all major battles," A. Judson Evans of the *Times-Dispatch* wrote facetiously, with obvious exaggeration.

"What about Joe Wheeler?" one Confederate wanted to know. "Have you ever heard of the Rockbridge Artillery?" said another. "I was present when Stonewall was shot; what about him?" a third interjected. "Ever hear of Pickett?"; "What about the navy?"; and so on. Freeman

answered them all, but still another wanted to be heard. "You know about the Crater? Right over there in Petersburg—five hundred South Carolinians blowed up in one night, and you ain't mentioned it!"

Dr. Freeman finally managed to introduce General Brown.

A notable event on the next day was the presentation at the Confederate Museum of the anchor of the *Virginia-Merrimac* to the Confederate Memorial Literary Society, which operates the museum. Miss Mary Maury Fitzgerald, grand-

daughter of Commodore Matthew Fontaine Maury made the presentation. Miss Sally Archer Anderson, president of the Confederate Memorial Literary Society, accepted the anchor for that organization. It was placed in the yard of the museum, where it can be seen today.

A bronze marker commemorating the inauguration of Jefferson Davis as Confederate president was dedicated at the Washington Monument in Capitol Square. The Davis inauguration had taken place in a pouring rain on February 22, 1862, with the crowd shivering under umbrellas. The speaker for the unveiling of the tablet seventy years later was Rosewell Page, brother of Thomas Nelson Page, and a state official. He read from his ambitious poem *The Iliads of the South*, a long series of verses occupying 26 "books" and 190 printed pages. The writing of poetry was hardly Mr. Page's forte. His lines on Jefferson Davis are typical of the whole:

> With Jefferson Davis, a State's Rights man,
> Provisional President, ere last four joined;
> Elected after Constitution framed,
> By all the States of the Confederacy.
> Experienced and eloquent in speech,
> Belonging to the ancient State's Rights school,
> And ever firmly set in his own ways.
> Right gallantly, he fought in Mexico;
> His statesmanship he learned from great Calhoun;
> In halls of Congress well he bore himself
> As Mississippi's leading senator:
> The Secretary of War he once had been;
> And popular when Pierce was President.
> In casemate manacled a martyr made,
> Vicarious sufferer for the South,
> He soon became; and has been since so deemed!
> Afraid to test Secession in the courts
> Lest it be legally by courts upheld,
> His foes dismissed the treasonable charge
> When Charles O'Connor [*sic*] and the rest appeared,
> And Horace Greeley joined in his bail bond!

The elderly warriors at the UCV convention did some high stepping at the grand ball the night of June 23 in the Grays' Armory. As Mary Binford Hobson wrote in the *Times-Dispatch*: "Spry and gallant as they were back in the days when their partners wore hoop skirts and pantaloons, these happy gentlemen swung their partners gaily along the Grand March, did some fancy jigging to the music of the old time fiddlers, and interrupted the square dancing to kiss the hands of the cheering spectators, or to chuck some of the pretty girls under the chin." There was life in the old boys yet.

The SCV held its grand ball at the armory the next night. An elaborate figure devised by Dr. William R. Dancey of Savannah, incoming commander-in-chief, took an hour and a half to run off, so intricate were the maneuvers. As usual the playing of "Dixie" elicited a storm of applause and shouts. Those were the days when the rousing Confederate song could be played without inhibitions.

The National Broadcasting Company came up with the idea of interviewing some of the old Confederates on the radio. The aged warriors entered into the activity with spirit—so much so, according to Joseph Bryan III, the Richmond author, that the show had to be cut short midway during one interview.

Bryan, whose grandfather, Joseph Bryan, served gallantly during the war as one of John S. Mosby's famous partisans, reports that the radio program began with a rendition of the Rebel yell by a group of a dozen veterans. Age had made their voices weak and thin, and one of the old gentlemen sought to compensate by giving so tremendous an effort that his suspenders snapped and his pants fell down.

Wade Arnold, handling the program for NBC, then opened an interview with "Uncle Charlie," a nonagenarian from New Orleans, last name unknown. Uncle Charlie reported that the uniform he was wearing had been made for him by his "Maw" when he enlisted and "jined Gen'l Beaurehgyahd."

Arnold sought to pursue the story of the uniform, but Uncle Charlie had other ideas. "Nemmine *mah* close," he said. "Ah'll tell you-all sump'n 'bout *women's* close!"

The script did not call for discourse on that subject, and Arnold attempted to get his guest back on track, but Uncle Charlie would have none of it. "They's a scandal, that's what!" he continued. "Ah mean short skirts!"

Again the announcer moved to change the topic without success. "No matter wheh you go," continued Uncle Charlie. "—on the street, in the theayter, in the sportin' house. . . ."

Major Crowley, Secret Dispatch Rider for Jefferson Davis, Is Distinguished Visitor

88-Year-Old Veteran Had Unusually Adventurous War Record.

Major John Crowley, of New Orleans, who served as secret dispatch rider for President Jefferson Davis during the war between the states, is one of the most interesting and distinguished veterans attending the reunion here.

The major says that he was at the White House of the Confederacy with President Davis at the time Winnie Davis was born, and that he was the first person outside of the family who kissed the infant. He also claims to have coined for her the famous sobriquet, "Daughter of the Confederacy."

The 88-year-old veteran had an unusually adventurous war record, since he crossed the Union lines thirty times disguised as a Negro girl. His first commission was given him by the Confederate president, he says, after he had presented himself to Mr. Davis dressed as a Negro girl with a tattered dress and market basket, his face and hands stained with walnut. President Davis was himself deceived and immediately added him to his couriers.

Epochal Commission.

The first commission of the major's was an epochal one. He was entrusted with a message to the British minister in Washington, whose aid the South sought to enlist. He made the hazardous trip of 1,200 miles on horseback, and it required twenty-nine days. Leaving Montgomery, he rode continuously for fifty-eight hours to Birmingham and was marooned in a swamp all night. Finally, he came into contact with the Union lines nine miles below Alexandria, Va. He had discarded the horse for a mule and rode into camp singing lustily, to all appearances a Negro girl. The Union officers who questioned him, were deceived and permitted "her" to go on.

Crowley delivered his message safely and then returned to Richmond, to which the Southern capitol had been removed. There he was rewarded with a captain's commission and assigned to Lee's headquarters. Afterwards he crossed the lines into Washington twenty-three times before his ruse was discovered.

He was sentenced to be shot by a drumhead court martial, but his youth aroused the sympathy of a group of Washington women, who prevailed upon Secretary of State Stanton to intervene and Lincoln commuted his death sentence to imprisonment at Camp Chase, Columbus, Ohio. There he contracted fever and when he returned to the South he was made brevet major.

Major Crowley was one of the guards who accompanied Jefferson Davis' body from New Orleans to Richmond for burial.

The major is a picturesque figure with his white hair and goatee, his Confederate uniform and sword and his cross of honor and other medals. He is unable to speak above a whisper due to a knife wound received several years ago from a member of an anarchist group in New Orleans.

Major John Crowley, of New Orleans, one of Jefferson Davis' secret couriers, was photographed on his arrival here to attend the Confederate reunion. He is shown with a United States flag, which he says was one of the first made by American women, following the Boston Tea Party. [News Leader photo by Dementi.]

—From the Richmond News Leader.

An Artist Catches the Notables at Confederate Reunion Events

Richmond Times-Dispatch cartoon by Foxo Reardon.

That did it. An on-the-air reference to a "sportin' house" was, in that era, scandalous beyond the pale. The interview was abruptly terminated.

The grand parade of the Confederate veterans, the last in history, passed along Richmond streets on Friday, June 24, as the Stars and Bars and other flags of the Confederacy fluttered from windows and were waved from sidewalks. There were lumps in many throats, including mine, as the procession passed, for it was realized by all that this scene could never be repeated. The aged participants who had served under Beauregard at Shiloh or charged Union breastworks with Hood had to make the trip in automobiles since they were no longer able to go on foot. A group of veterans waved a sign calling for repeal of the Eighteenth Amendment, which brought laughter and cheers.

The numerous bands played Southern airs, with "Dixie" the most popular of all. Members of the Richmond Light Infantry Blues, a historic military unit going back for its origins to 1789,

were dashingly impressive in their Napoleonic dress uniforms, refurbished with new facing and shakos. They were led by Major Mills F. Neal, their longtime commander. Also in the parade were the Richmond Grays and the Howitzers with their horses and field pieces. Officials of the SCV, UDC, and CSMA occupied prominent places in the line. Other patriotic groups were there, including the 40-and-8 of World War I days. There was applause for all marching units.

The Confederate veterans blew kisses to the ladies and smiled at the children as the procession passed. An especially lively participant was Major John Crowley, a Louisiana Tiger who had served during the war as a rider to carry secret dispatches for President Jefferson Davis. Holding tightly to the banner of the South, he insisted on riding part of the time astride the hood of the car in which Virginia's adjutant-general, S. Gardner Waller, was traveling. But when the parade passed the statues on Monument Avenue, Major Crowley dismounted and saluted each one. "Ten thousand men like that could lick any army in the world," said General Waller. The major was deemed "a gallant figure by all," the newspaper account declared.

The Formation and Line of March for Today's Parade Here

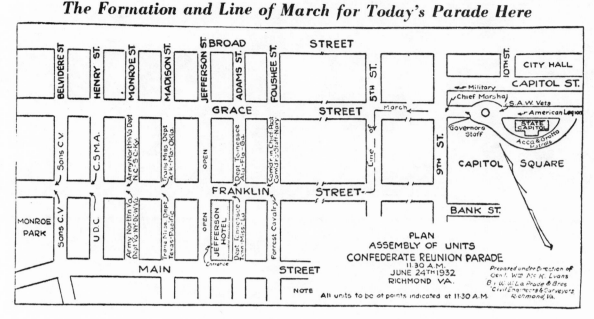

PLAN
ASSEMBLY OF UNITS
CONFEDERATE REUNION PARADE
11.30 A.M.
JUNE 24TH 1932
RICHMOND VA.

NOTE All units to be at points indicated at 11.30 A.M.

Prepared under Direction of
Gen'l W^m Mc. K. Evans
B. W. W. La Prade & Bros
Civil Engineers & Surveyors
Richmond, Va.

While in the city for the reunion the aged veterans were well looked after by the local citizenry. Richmond's young ladies in particular delighted in bestowing attention upon the old soldiers. Indeed, so smitten by the charms of one such hostess was a veteran from Tennessee that after returning home he wrote requesting a photograph of the lady, and upon receiving it, proposed matrimony:

I feel as if the Lord had something to do with our meeting. When I met you you seemed to be the one I have been looking for. I feel that we could get along fine and my lawyer is working to get my pension now. Write quick. I want to know what you think of being Mrs. I——— instead of Miss C———. There was a woman in Biloxi Miss met a man, talked and then they were married in the parade.

Write and tell me when and where the next reunion will be, as I never hear anything like that, and I want to meet you there, if not before.

Answer quick and a long letter, and be sure and tell me how it will suit you to have your name changed You have worn the C——— name long enough.

Give your mother my warm regards.

Your true Friend
J. A. I———

P.S. If you get letters from any one concerning mine and your case pay no attention to it.

The young lady in question, though flattered, wrote back that she was not ready to consider matrimony just yet.

One of the last acts of the forty-second annual reunion of UCV was to elect General Homer T. Atkinson of Petersburg commander-in-chief, succeeding General De Saussure. General Atkinson was the last survivor of the gallant group of old men and boys who had saved Petersburg in the battle of June 9, 1864. He was only fifteen at the time. Subsequently he managed to join the army, apparently by giving his age as seventeen. In 1865 he was commissioned second lieutenant in Company B, 19th regiment of Mississippi Infantry. Later Atkinson was captured; he refused to take

the oath of allegiance and remained in prison until midsummer 1865.

Many of the delegates to the convention left for their homes on Saturday morning, June 25, as they did not feel up to the planned side trip to Washington aboard a special train. Events during the four days in Richmond had left a goodly number exhausted. The relatively hardy minority took the train to the nation's capital for a series of events, notably a parade down Pennsylvania Avenue. It was headed, spectacularly, by four veterans on horseback who had ridden with Forrest. They made a brave show. In the line as it moved past the reviewing stand, in addition to the Confederates, were several military bands, troops of cavalry, blue jackets, Marine and Coast Guard units, veterans of various wars, Boy Scouts, and even the Daughters of Job.

President Herbert Hoover's failure to review the parade was a serious disappointment. Perhaps exhausted by his trials and tribulations during the deepening depression, the president had departed for his camp on the Rapidan, and Secretary of the Navy Charles Francis Adams, Jr., did the honors. Adams was an appropriate choice, since his father, the New England historian, had been one of Robert E. Lee's staunchest defenders, saying that if he had been in Lee's place in 1861, he would have done what Lee did.

The program of events in and around Washington included a basket picnic on the field of Manassas or Bull Run, the placing of a wreath on the tomb of the Unknown Soldier at Arlington by General De Saussure, and another on the Confederate Monument by Dr. George R. Tabor, former commander-in-chief of the Sons of Confederate Veterans. As the final event the U.S. Marine Band gave a concert.

After 1932 there would not be enough survivors of the Civil War to hold another Confederate convention that could be called a major reunion in the usual sense. A gathering billed as the final reunion of the United Confederate Veterans took place in Norfolk, Virginia, in late May and early June, 1951. Only three veterans, aged 104 and 105, out of the twelve or more who were still living, managed to attend. The meeting was held in conjunction with the convention of the Sons of Confederate Veterans, hundreds of whom were present.

The three members of UCV who came were William Joshua Bush of Fitzgerald, Georgia; William D. Townsend of Olla, Louisiana; and John Salling of Slant, Virginia. All three were "generals." General Bush, 105, was the liveliest. "I can hear good, I can see good, I can taste good, and I can kiss any damn woman who wants to be kissed," said he. His wife felt it necessary to admonish him several times: "Hush, Daddy, stop that cussing."

Soon after the UCV's convention in Richmond adjourned, I wrote a series of editorials in the *Times-Dispatch* suggesting that the Blue and the Gray hold a final get-together at Washington, D.C., in 1935. I then dispatched a letter to the UCV's adjutant and chief-of-staff at Nashville, in which I advanced this proposal. I expressed the hope that the GAR would withdraw its recent stipulation that no meeting could be held with the UCV unless it left its flags behind. Without replying to me, the official announced in the press that he had received my proposal and that he had no intention of accepting it. He interpreted it, incorrectly, to mean that I wanted him to "plead with" the GAR to let the "Rebs" carry their banners. His summary rejection of the idea of a last joint reunion seemed to end all hope for such a meeting, at least for the foreseeable future.

But it developed that a committee had been appointed in Pennsylvania to arrange a joint reunion at Gettysburg in 1938 to be held on the seventy-fifth anniversary of the battle. Such a reunion had been held there in 1913 on the fiftieth anniversary. Five months after my suggestion for a Washington reunion was rejected, the UCV met at Amarillo, Texas, and voted unanimously to accept the invitation to Gettysburg, since the members had been assured by the commission that they could wave their flags at

Dan Clawin Winnsett, of the Confederate Home at Big Rock, Ark., showing Richmond Boy Scout Lodwell Fourqurean how he blows a bugle. The scouts are great favorites with the veterans and other visitors, and their services are invaluable.

—From the Richmond Times-Dispatch.

will. Yet only two days later the commander-in-chief of the GAR proclaimed to all and sundry that it would never allow the UCV to display its banners on such an occasion. The UCV, however, was assured at its Jackson, Mississippi, meeting the next year that the Starry Cross could be flown at Gettysburg, and it voted once more to accept. This came despite the objections of one Johnny Reb who declared that "they waited thirty-five years to invite us, and I ain't having nothin' to do with them Yankees until they pay us for the property they destroyed in the war."

It appeared at last, despite these ups and downs, that the thing was settled. But the GAR was yet to be heard from. Its convention met for two days behind closed doors and came up with the dictum that "only the flag of the United States of America" could be flown at Gettysburg. It seemed that this ended all hope, since neither the UCV not the GAR was to meet again before the summer of 1938.

At that point somebody passed a miracle. Only those on the inside understood how it was accomplished, and maybe they didn't understand it either. At all events both groups showed up at Gettysburg. One argument that apparently was used had it that it really wasn't a joint reunion, and that the Yanks and Rebs were simply accepting an invitation from the State of Pennsylvania to attend anniversary ceremonies, all expenses paid by the U.S. government. Until they got there, nobody knew whether there would be a second Battle of Gettysburg when the Southerners flaunted their banners.

Such apprehensions turned out to be completely unjustified. Some eighteen hundred Northern and Southern veterans went to Gettysburg, and they had a rousing and altogether pleasant time. The reunion lasted for eight days, and the old boys enjoyed themselves hugely. They sat under the trees, exchanging good-natured gibes, while the Confederate and United States flags flapped in the breeze, and the bands played "Dixie" and "Yankee Doodle."

Prohibition by then was a thing of the past, and five cases of whiskey were placed at the disposal of the veterans. Their capacity had been grossly underestimated, for the usquebaugh was exhausted in short order, thanks primarily to the elbowbending prowess of the Southern contingent. Those in charge of arrangements appeared to think that a small beaker containing a teaspoon of whiskey would be adequate, but this brought hoots of dismay. One of the boys in gray snorted: "That ain't even a good sniff, much less a drink!" An airplane was dispatched for additional supplies, and it returned with twenty-two more cases. This supply, too, gave out, and fifteen additional cases were found to be necessary. One elderly delegate, aged 104, was picked up suffering from acute alcoholism, but there appear to have been no other serious casualties. As the veterans prepared to depart, they requested a small flask apiece "to see them home." Their request was granted.

John M. Claypool, UCV commander-in-chief, said: "I've just been tickled to death. I've been to lots of reunions but never anything like this. I knew it would be good, but it turned out better than anything I could conceive." Overton H. Mennet, GAR commander-in-chief, echoed these sentiments, saying that members of his organization "had the time of our lives." There had been similarly amicable joint reunions in the past between the Blue and the Gray, but none so significant as this, for there could never be another. Only a few years more would pass before the last of the Civil War veterans would go to his reward.

It was especially moving that this final meeting should have taken place on the field where some of these men had met in mortal combat three-quarters of a century earlier. National unity had been forged at Santiago and Manila Bay, in Belleau Wood and at St. Mihiel; and now the men who had faced one another in deadly combat in the great Civil War had decided that the war was over. The Gettysburg reunion of 1938 was deeply symbolic for the nation.

The goodwill generated there carried over to the United Daughters of the Confederacy and the Daughters of the Union. Mrs. Charles E. Bolling, UDC president-general, invited Mrs. Louis Ward Watkins, president-general of the DOU, to be her guest at the unveiling of a bust of Jefferson Davis at Montgomery, Alabama, in 1940. Mrs. Watkins expressed deep regret over her inability to accept, saying in part: "Although you doubtless will have

many flowers as gifts from admirers from all over the country, please wear the corsage which I send with my loving greetings sometime during the convention." Mrs. Watkins was able to attend the UDC's Los Angeles convention the next year, and was a much-feted guest.

That exchange was one more bit of evidence that the animosities between the sections were virtually a thing of the past. The commander-in-chief of the GAR had actually said in 1935 that the Confederate veterans ought to be placed on the federal pension rolls!

I myself received an unexpected accolade from the UCV chief of staff who had scornfully rejected my suggestion in 1935 for a last reunion of the Northern and Southern veterans. To my astonishment he wrote, after the Gettysburg reunion, inviting me to accept a position as "historian-general of the United Confederate Veterans, with the rank of brigadier-general." I had supposed that nobody under 85 years of age could be accorded the rank of general in the UCV, and was greatly flattered by the invitation. I felt unable to accept such awesome responsibilities, however, and I declined.

The amount of interest today, both in this country and overseas, in the events of the Civil War is astonishing. There are some eighty-four active Civil War round tables which meet regularly and study the conflict of the 1860s intensively. These round tables have an average membership of about fifty, so that there are more than four thousand members overall. The first Civil War Round Table was founded in Chicago in 1940, and the organizations are now scattered all over the United States, with descendants of both Union and Confederate soldiers as members. There is a round table in London, whose meetings members attend from throughout England. Another meets in Melbourne, Australia, and still another in Winnipeg, Canada. The Confederate Historical Society of Brussels, Belgium, is closely affiliated with the American round tables. There are even Civil War round tables in two penal institutions—the Virginia State Penitentiary at Richmond, and the federal prison at Hagerstown, Maryland. The

inmates study the events of the war in great detail, and they have regular speakers who are specialists. When one of these wrote the Virginia penitentiary inquiring as to when it would be most convenient for him to appear, the head of the Round Table wrote back: "Just come any time; we'll be here."

There was a striking example in London, on the one-hundredth anniversary of Lee's surrender at Appomattox, of the vitality of the Civil War tradition. On the front page of *The Times* of London, April 9, 1965, the following paid advertisements appeared side by side:

ARMY OF NORTHERN VIRGINIA—In affectionate remembrance of Robert Edward Lee, General CSA, and the brave men who surrendered with him at Appomattox Court House on April 9, 1865.

In memory of those who stood at Appomattox—and those who died before—9th April, 1865.

On a less serious note were the amusing antics of a comical radio character, Senator Beauregard Claghorn, who appeared on Fred Allen's Sunday evening program during the 1940s. Claghorn, a caricature of politicians, was a professional Southerner and worshipper of all things Confederate. A typical utterance was: "In college Ah was voted the member of the senior class most likely to secede, and Ah was graduated magnolia cum laude." Also: "When in New York Ah only dance at the Cotton Club. The only dance Ah do is the Virginia Reel. The only train Ah ride is the Chattanooga Choo Choo. When Ah pass Grant's tomb Ah shut both eyes. Ah never go to the Yankee Stadium, and Ah won't even go to the Polo Grounds unless a southpaw's pitchin'." While some Southern politicians were and are almost as ridiculous as Senator Claghorn, he was an obvious caricature. A few of the characteristics he displayed can be traced to certain individuals below the Mason and Dixon Line, but none is quite as absurd as Claghorn.

Some of these public characters still evidence undue antagonism toward the North. And there is misunderstanding in that part of the country concerning prevailing attitudes in the South. An example is seen in an article by Horace Sutton entitled "Sunbelt vs. Frostbelt: A Second Civil War?" in the *Saturday Review* for April 15, 1978. Mr. Sutton writes: "One hundred and seventeen

Old Warriors Line Up for a Reunion Inspection Here

years after the outbreak of the Civil War, we remain a nation where part of the country waves and reveres the flag of the Confederate breakaway States and still sings 'Dixie' as if it were 'Onward Christian Soldiers.' ''

This is a considerable overstatement, if Mr. Sutton means that the South "waves and reveres" the Confederate banner in a chauvinistic and excessive manner, and that is apparently what he does mean. A few Ku Klux types do display the flag in this fashion, but they are an infinitesimal minority; and college students are sometimes wont to brandish it at athletic contests. But I am happy to report that the great majority of white Southerners have stopped displaying the Confederate flag except on anniversaries related to the Civil War or on the birthdays of Confederate heroes. No black would think of displaying it, of course, since the blacks regard it as a symbol of slavery. And, indeed, there is no warrant today for flying the flag of a long-defunct government, except when special occasions make it appropriate.

"Dixie" is being played less and less, since the blacks object to it so strongly, even though Abraham Lincoln requested that it be played on at least two occasions. Mr. Sutton's statement that it arouses emotions below the Mason and Dixon Line like those caused by the singing of "Onward Christian Soldiers" does not accord with the facts. The song is regarded in the South as a rousing battle tune, which it undoubtedly is, and as evoking nostalgic recollections of a long-gone era; but I can't imagine where Sutton picked up his remarkably outdated notions. They may have been correct for 1890 or 1910, but certainly they are not for today. It is well known that Southerners showed a greater eagerness to enlist for the country's defense in both world wars than citizens of any other section.

"Dixie" has been to the South what the "Marseillaise" is to France, according to one

observer. Most Southerners are familiar with one or two verses and the chorus, but it appears probable that few have seen the full text, as originally written. "Dixie" or "Dixie's Land," the original title, was composed in 1859 by Daniel Decatur Emmett, a native of Ohio whose father was a Virginian. "I count myself a Southerner," he said. Emmett, who had composed various other songs, including "Old Dan Tucker," wrote "Dixie" on a rainy weekend in New York City, when he was asked to produce what was called a walk-around for the next day's Bryant Minstrels, of which he was a member. It was an instant hit, and "soon everybody was whistling it." The song was on the program in 1861 at the swearing-in of Jefferson Davis as president of the Confederate States of America at Montgomery. It became immensely popular at once throughout the South. The song's strains never failed to stir the enthusiasm of soldiers and civilians in the region.

There are several theories as to the origin of the term *Dixie*. Some said it was a corruption of the phrase *Mason and Dixon's Line*. Others traced it to ten-dollar bills issued by a New Orleans bank, which bore the word *dix*—French for ten—on one side. These bills were popularly known as "dixies" and the area in which they circulated "the land of Dixies." Still another theory goes back to a beloved eighteenth-century slaveowner on Manhattan Island named Dixy of Dixie, whose slaves were forced to move to the South, but longed for their old home in the North. They are said to have begun singing of "Dixie's Land" as a heaven on earth. There is no consensus as to which of these theories is correct; in fact the explanation may be found elsewhere.

The words of the original song, taken here from the official program of the UCV's reunion in 1896, are horrendous doggerel. Since it was written for a minstrel show, this was to be expected. The original has since been altered and improved in various subsequent versions, but there is no agreement today as to the precise wording. In view of the song's importance in the history of the Civil War, and of Confederate reunions and other such observances, the full text, as written in 1859, should be known.

DIXIE'S LAND

I wish I was in de land ob cotton
'Cimmon seed and sandy bottom,
Look a-way, look 'way, a-way, Dixie Land.
In Dixie's Land where I was born in
Early on one frosty mornin'
Look a-way, look 'way, a-way, Dixie Land.

Den I wish I was in Dixie,
CHORUS—Hooray! Hooray!
In Dixie's Land we'll took our stand,
To lib' an' die in Dixie,
A-way, a-way, away down South in Dixie.

Old missus marry Will, de weaber,
William was a gay deceaber;
When he put his arm around 'er,
He look as fierce as a forty-pounder.
Hooray! Hooray! etc.

His face was sharp like a butcher's cleaver
But dat did not seem to greab 'er;
Will, run away, missus took a decline, O,
Her face was de color ob bacon rhine, O.
Hooray! Hooray! etc.

While missus libbed she libbed in clober,
When she died she died all ober;
How could she act such a foolish part, O,
An marry a man to break her heart, O.
Hooray! Hooray! etc.

Buckwheat cakes and stony batter,
Makes you fat or a little fatter;
Here's a health to de next old missus,
An' all de gals dat wants to kiss us.
Hooray! Hooray! etc.

Now if you want to drive 'way sorrow,
Come and hear dis song tomorrow;
Den hoe it down an' scratch yer grabble,
To Dixie's Lane I'm bound to trabble.
Hooray! Hooray! etc.

"Dixie" was still being played frequently in the South during the 1960s, when the centennial of the Civil War was observed all over the United States.

In 1961 President John F. Kennedy appointed Professor James I. Robertson Jr., then of the University of Iowa, as executive director of the Civil War Centennial Commission. He supervised and coordinated the programs, and worked for several years with 34 state centennial commissions plus 275 local centennial committees and other

Confederate Reunion Ends in Brilliant Parade

—*From the Richmond Times-Dispatch and Richmond News Leader.*

organizations. Many special publications were issued, battles were reenacted, exhibits were mounted, and other ceremonies were held. Robertson was given the Harry S. Truman Award in 1962 as the nation's foremost Civil War historian, an award unrelated to the centennial observance.

Focusing attention on the events of the 1860s was an educational experience for the people of this country. Since a century had passed, citizens in both the North and the South were able to view events of the war objectively, and there were almost no rancorous outbursts, such as had occurred in earlier decades. The relaxed atmosphere in which the one-hundredth anniversary of the war was observed is epitomized in the comment of J. Ambler Johnston, chairman of the Richmond centennial commission. "The right side won," said he, "but the other side was nicer."

Myths concerning the war and its aftermath sprang up in the South during the decades that followed Appomattox, and survived well into the twentieth century. It was not always easy to know what was fact and what was fiction. One incredible myth—at least I take it to be such—emerged in recent years for the first time into the modern world. This had to do with Stonewall Jackson, and the unbelievable allegation was that he begat an illegitimate child in his youth. The gossip appears as an addendum to Holmes Alexander's recent book, *The Hidden Years of Stonewall Jackson*, and was broadcast by the Associated Press. Alexander evidently was quite unsure of the rumor's authenticity, and he played it down, He had gleaned it from an earlier book by General Ezra Ayers Carman, who also relegated it to an addendum. One can only conclude that a straight-laced, hard-praying puritan such as Jackson is about as unlikely a father of an illegitimate child as one could well imagine. No name, sex, or birth date is given in any account.

The Civil War is fairly vivid today in the minds

of many. This is seen, for example, in the fact that there is a continuing demand for authentic uniforms of both Union and Confederate soldiers. A Massachusetts couple and a Virginia couple, both in their thirties, are turning out these uniforms in large lots for sale at from $300 to $450 each. The same thing is being done at various other places, both North and South.

What was the South fighting for from 1861 to 1865?

There are people today who believe that the South's primary objective was to preserve slavery in the region—and that the North's primary aim was to abolish it. This is a vast oversimplification.

It was the controversy over slavery, rather than a desire to perpetuate it, that finally brought secession and war. The antebellum South was basically a community, with common traditions, beliefs, and aspirations. It was being thrown increasingly on the defensive by attacks from the North, and its political and economic leadership became united in an effort to protect its institutions from these assaults. Numerous Southerners realized that slavery could not survive indefinitely, but events were pushing them into a posture of defending it, along with pretty much everything else in the region.

As intersectional tensions escalated, fire-eaters in the deep South, led by those in Charleston, were leaning more and more toward secession. On December 20, 1860, South Carolina's convention voted without a single dissenter to secede, and six other Southern states soon followed the Palmetto State out of the Union.

The upper South still sought a peaceful solution. Virginia led in calling for a convention in Washington on February 4, 1861, in the hope that somehow the widening breach could be healed. But the seven states that had seceded ignored the gathering, and it was a failure. In April came the bombardment of Fort Sumter. President Lincoln called for seventy-five thousand men, including a due proportion of Southerners, to put down the "rebellion." The Southern states refused to comply, and the die was cast.

Would defeat of the North in the war have been in the best interests of the South? Viewed in the calm perspective of today, it would seem that a decisive Confederate victory at Antietam or Gettysburg, followed by recognition of the Confederate government by Great Britain and France, and termination of hostilities, with the South victorious, would not have profited the Southern states in the long run.

They would have achieved their independence at least temporarily, would have avoided the ordeal of Reconstruction, and would probably have abolished slavery in due time. But there would have remained the ever-present danger of a renewal of hostilities by a larger, wealthier, more heavily industrialized and more populous North, licking its wounds and yearning for revenge. Even if that had not occurred, and the two sections had managed to remain at peace under separate governments, the breaking up of the Union would have been a tragedy. The intersectional animosities and antagonisms of other days have died, and we are a united country. Furthermore, in a world wherein Kaiser Wilhelm II, Adolf Hitler, and Josef Stalin and his successors have threatened the very existence of the United States, the peril to this nation and to the free world would have been much greater if this country had been cut in two. As a result of such considerations, I wrote in a magazine article some years ago that "perhaps the gods were kind when the gray wave spent itself on the scarred crest of Cemetery Hill, when Gettysburg was lost and Vicksburg fell."

The old men who gathered at Richmond in 1932, almost the last of the war's survivors, brought back memories of sanguinary clashes at Shiloh and Chancellorsville, Lookout Mountain and Brice's Cross Roads, Atlanta and Appomattox. Both the Blue and the Gray had much to be proud of in the record they made. On both sides there was gallantry of the highest order. And in the fires that raged during the four years of desperate combat was forged a stronger America, to confront whatever looming dangers the future might hold.

II

AN ALBUM OF PHOTOGRAPHS

Scene from an earlier reunion in Richmond, probably in the
late 1910s or early 1920s. A city policeman escorts two ageing
ex-Confederates across an intersection on Broad Street.
Courtesy Richmond Newspapers, Inc.

This photograph of Confederate veterans lined up for
review along Grace Street would appear to date
from the 1900s or 1910s.
Courtesy Richmond Newspapers, Inc.

The Home for Confederate Women, dedicated during the
1932 Reunion. Note streetcar tracks on Shepherd Street.
Courtesy Dementi-Foster Studios.

The official welcome party greets General C. A. De Saussure of Nashville, Tennessee, upon his arrival in Richmond for the Reunion. Left to right, Brigadier General S. Gardner Waller, adjutant-general of Virginia; Major Robert T. Barton, general chairman of the local reunion committee (in white suit); General De Saussure; and General W. B. Freeman, of Richmond, former UCV commander-in-chief and father of Douglas Southall Freeman. Behind General De Saussure is General Richard A. Snead, of Oklahoma. General W. McK. Evans of Virginia (wearing straw hat) stands behind General Freeman.

Courtesy Dementi-Foster Studios.

General C. A. De Saussure. Behind him is Virginia State Senator
Henry T. Wickham.
Courtesy Richmond Newspapers, Inc.

Friendly game at Soldiers' Home. Note well-used
spittoon at bottom, right.
Courtesy Dementi-Foster Studios.

A Confederate veteran points with his cane at one
of the cannons used in the defense of Fort Sumter,
on display at Soldiers' Home in Richmond,
while others look on.
Courtesy Dementi-Foster Studios.

What is so unusual about this photograph of two Confederate veterans
seated on a bench at Soldiers' Home during the Reunion? (The old soldiers,
in town for the Reunion, are General L. H. Limrick, of Oak Ridge, Louisiana,
and General J. K. Leillard, of Dallas, Texas.) Merely that the shrub growing in front of the window behind them is a marijuana plant!
Courtesy Dementi-Foster Studios.

Five of the thirteen residents of Lee Camp, UCV, still living at the time of the 1932 Reunion are shown in this photograph. Flanking them are members of General W. McK. Evans's staff. Left to right, Marcellus Wright, Lieutenant M. M. Wallace, Augustine Royall, Peter J. White, Andrew Krouse, General Evans, Mike Wade (holding flag), Colonel Frank Wells, and Major Arthur Bell.

Courtesy Dementi-Foster Studios.

One of the prime attractions to be seen at the Soldiers' Home in Richmond
was the stuffed carcass of Old Sorrel, Stonewall Jackson's favorite war horse.
Here General J. C. Smith, of Meigs, Georgia, who fought under Jackson at
the Battle of Chancellorsville, admires his old chieftain's charger.
Courtesy Dementi-Foster Studios.

J. D. Dowling, of Ringo, Georgia, and Miss Florence Baynes, of Richmond,
secretary of Lee Camp, UCV.
Courtesy Dementi-Foster Studios.

Tennessee, North Carolina, and Virginia are represented in this
Reunion photograph. Left to right, Generals S. A. Hughey, S. A.
Hildebrand, A. Sims Aiken, and Gilbert Harris.
Courtesy Richmond Newspapers, Inc.

Unfortunately, no identification exists for these four
distinguished-looking veterans attending the 1932 Reunion.
Courtesy Richmond Newspapers, Inc.

Before an artillery piece of the Army of Northern Virginia,
Reunion members compare notes. Clearly the cannon ball
was designed for use in a coastal defense mortar.
Courtesy Dementi-Foster Studios.

These two aged residents of Soldiers' Home, one of them
with wooden leg, raise the Confederate colors.
Courtesy Dementi-Foster Studios.

Distinguished visitors at afternoon ceremonies at Maymont, the Dooley estate in Richmond. Left to right, Colonel George Mason Lee, Mrs. Daisy Lester Avery, General G. F. H. Howell, Mrs. Fitzhugh Lee, Colonel Fitzhugh Lee, U.S.A., General Ezra Atkinson, Brigadier General S. Gardner Waller, Colonel R. Keith Compson.

Courtesy Richmond Newspapers, Inc.

Guests at luncheon given by John Stewart Bryan at Laburnum in honor of
the grandsons of Robert E. Lee and Ulysses S. Grant. Bottom, left to right,
Major General Lytle Brown, chief of engineers, U.S.A., Colonel Ulysses S.
Grant III, U.S.A., Dr. George Bolling Lee, Tazewell M. Carrington. Top, left
to right, Dr. Douglas Southall Freeman, W. Brydon Tennant, J. Ambler
Johnston, Spencer Carter, Jonathan Bryan, John Stewart Bryan.
Courtesy Dementi-Foster Studios.

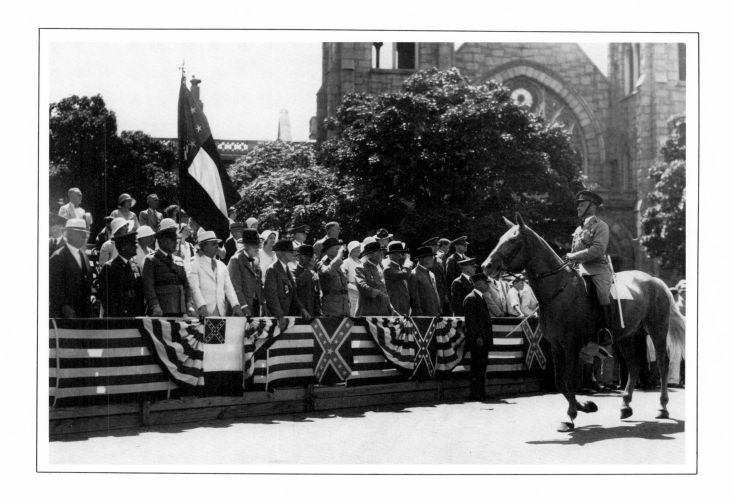

The Last Parade: The official party at the reviewing stand accepts the salute
of the mounted Army captain (note sword) as the parade passes in review.
Courtesy Dementi-Foster Studios.

The Last Parade: The newly elected commander-in-chief of the United
Confederate Veterans, General Homer A. Atkinson, rear seat, left, and the
retiring commander-in-chief, General C. A. De Saussure, rear seat, right,
receive the plaudits of the crowd.

Courtesy Richmond Newspapers, Inc.

The Last Parade: The Richmond Blues pass the statue of Stonewall Jackson
at Boulevard and Monument Avenue.
Courtesy Dementi-Foster Studios.

The Last Parade: The Richmond Blues lead the military parade as they
swing past the Lee Statue at Lee Circle on Monument Avenue.
Courtesy Richmond Newspapers, Inc.

Farewell to Richmond. Scene at Broad Street Station as a contingent
of Confederate veterans and admirers prepare to board a special train
that will carry them from the onetime Confederate capital on to the
nation's capital in Washington, where they will take part in yet another parade.

Courtesy Richmond Newspapers, Inc.

Although the 1932 Richmond Reunion was the last major gathering of the veterans of the Confederate Army and Navy, additional reunions continued to take place. In 1938, both Confederate and Union veterans participated in a final joint reunion of the opposing armies at Gettysburg. In this scene (which may be from an earlier reunion at Gettysburg) the Blue and the Gray join each other for a session in the Confederate area of the encampment. As was true seventy-five years earlier, the numerical odds would appear to favor the Union Army.

Courtesy Richmond Newspapers, Inc.

III

RICHMOND MAGAZINE,

June, 1932, containing the Official
Program for the 42nd Annual Confederate
Reunion, Richmond, Virginia

This facsimile reproduction of *Richmond Magazine* for June, 1932, the official program for the Reunion, is complete except for certain pages containing advertisements and photographs of Reunion officials. It is reprinted through the courtesy of the Richmond Chamber of Commerce.

RICHMOND
M·A·G·A·Z·I·N·E

HOFFBAUER'S MURAL OF LEE AND HIS GENERALS
© CONFEDERATE MEMORIAL INSTITUTE

OFFICIAL PROGRAM
42ND ANNUAL
CONFEDERATE
REUNION
—
JUNE, 1932
35 CENTS

Greetings From
Governor Pollard and Mayor Bright

NO OTHER State of the Old Confederacy owes more to the Confederate Veterans than does Virginia. Happily, this Commonwealth has not forgotten the defenders who hurried to her aid when she was in need, nor will she forget so long as her people remain true to the finer traditions of the Old Dominion.

As Governor of the Commonwealth of Virginia, I bid you Veterans, Sons of Veterans and Members of the Confederated Southern Memorial Association a hearty welcome. The Commonwealth is yours for the Forty-second Annual Reunion. May your stay within her borders prove equally as pleasant as this opportunity afforded Virginia to play host to such a gathering.

—JOHN GARLAND POLLARD,
Governor of Virginia.

Governor John Garland Pollard   Dementi Photo

Mayor J. Fulmer Bright   Dementi Photo

RICHMOND, in whose sacred soil rests the bodies of those valiant defenders of seventy years ago and upon whose avenues have been erected lasting memorials to the valor of the Confederate soldier, deems it an exceptional privilege to welcome the United Confederate Veterans, the Sons of Confederate Veterans and members of the Confederated Southern Memorial Association.

It is peculiarly fitting that the Forty-second Annual Confederate Reunion should be held here upon the seventieth anniversary of the great campaigns waged in defense of Richmond. It is my sincere hope that the hospitality that brightened the life of the soldiers in 1862 will be found in every Richmond home throughout the four days of the Reunion. Having risen from the ashes of 1865, Richmond is happy in that you, representatives from every section of the South, are here to join in her thanksgiving and to partake of the hospitality she so gladly extends upon this occasion.

—J. FULMER BRIGHT,
Mayor of Richmond.

RICHMOND MAGAZINE

PUBLISHED MONTHLY BY THE RICHMOND CHAMBER OF COMMERCE

W. H. SCHWARZSCHILD, President   **MASON MANGHUM**, Executive Vice-President

J. MALCOLM BRIDGES, Editor   **CHRISTIAN MUNT**, Business Manager and Assistant Editor

VOLUME 18   **JUNE, 1932**   **NUMBER 12**

CONTRIBUTORS TO THIS ISSUE

The following distinguished historians, representing the foremost authorities of Virginia on Confederate history, co-operated with the editors of RICHMOND in making this Reunion issue possible:

Dr. H. J. Eckenrode, historian for the Virginia State Conservation and Development Commission, contributed the story of *Richmond's Battlefield Parks* and served as advisory editor for this number. Dr. Eckenrode was appointed State Historian for Virginia in 1927. He is the author of *History of Virginia During the Reconstruction*, *Separation of Church and State in Virginia*, *The Revolution in Virginia*, *Life of Nathan B. Forrest, Told in Story* (textbook), *Jefferson Davis* and other works.

Dr. Arthur Kyle Davis, of Petersburg, who contributed the story on *Petersburg's Three Hundred Days*, is president of Southern College and widely known as a historian. He is the author of *Three Centuries of an Old Virginia Town*, *Virginia's War History*; a former chairman of Virginia's War History Commission; editor of *Quarterly Supplements, Calendars and Reports in Virginia Historical Magazine*, *Virginians of Distinguished Service in the World War*, *Virginia War History in Newspaper Clippings*, and other works.

Dr. Douglas S. Freeman, editor of the *Richmond News Leader*, contributed the article, *The Confederate Tradition of Richmond*. He is widely known as an orator and historian. His works include *Reports on Virginia Taxation*, *Robert E. Lee*, and numerous studies in Confederate military history. Dr. Freeman will appear as one of the principal speakers in connection with the Forty-second Annual Confederate Reunion.

Dr. Richard Heath Dabney, whose story, *A Sample of Lee's Strategy*, appears in this issue, is professor of History at the University of Virginia. He is the author of numerous works, including *The Causes of the French Revolution*, *John Randolph, A Character Sketch*, and miscellaneous reviews. Dr. Dabney ranks high among the foremost historians of Virginia.

Dr. H. R. McIlwaine, Virginia State Librarian, contributed the article dealing with documents and other objects of special Confederate interest housed in the Library here. He is the author of *The Struggle of Protestant Dissenters for Religious Toleration in Virginia*; directed the notable work in connection with the publication of the Journal of the Virginia House of Burgesses, and is a member of the American Library Association, the American Historical Association, and the Virginia Historical Society.

CONTENTS

CONTRIBUTORS TO THIS ISSUE

The following distinguished historians, representing the foremost authorities of Virginia on Confederate history, co-operated with the editors of RICHMOND in making this Reunion issue possible:

Clifford Millard, of Norfolk, is one of the outstanding historians of the world on Confederate naval history. In his article, *Defenses and Defenders of Hampton Roads*, he has made use of much material gathered as a result of exhaustive research conducted personally in that area.

Col. H. L. Landers, U. S. A., of the Army War College, contributed the story entitled, *When the Tide Flowed Around the Capital*. He has made a comprehensive study of the Seven Days' campaign around Richmond and has written a monograph of 50,000 words on the subject. He is an officer of high distinction, gifted with the technique of historical research and the ability to write.

Allen W. Moger, whose story, *The Granary of the Confederacy*, comes as another feature of this issue, is a member of the History Department of Washington and Lee University. Like Mr. Millard, Colonel Landers, and Dr. Davis, he is thoroughly familiar with the section of which he writes. Other members of the faculty of Washington and Lee University have also rendered the editors of this issue invaluable assistance.

Thomas Lomax Hunter, author of the article on Fredericksburg and surrounding battlefields, is a distinguished attorney residing at King George, Va. His daily column, *As It Appears to the Cavalier*, is one of the outstanding features of the *Richmond Times-Dispatch*.

Miss Mary Maury Fitzgerald has contributed the article dealing with the women of the Confederacy. She is a granddaughter of Commodore Matthew Fontaine Maury and makes her home in Richmond, where she has written various historical articles, many of which have appeared in former issues of this publication.

Earle Lutz, author of *Raids on Richmond*, is a veteran Richmond newspaper man, now serving on the editorial staff of the *Richmond News Leader*. He served with distinction in the recent war and is the author of *The 110th Infantry in the World War*. Like Miss Fitzgerald, Mr. Lutz has been a regular contributor to RICHMOND for several years.

RICHMOND MAGAZINE is published monthly by the Advertising Committee of the Richmond Chamber of Commerce. Subscription rates: One year in the United States and possessions, $1.50; foreign, $2.00; payable in advance. Subscriptions should be mailed to Circulation Manager, P. O. Box 1536, Richmond, Va.

Communications to RICHMOND when free from political tone or religious prejudice, and signed by a responsible person will be published in the columns of this magazine.

Entered as second class matter July 13, 1914, at the Postoffice at Richmond, Va., under Act of March 3, 1879.

Copyright 1932.

Federal Troops Entering Richmond, April 3, 1865

AFTER the Confederate troops had burned and evacuated Richmond on Sunday night, early on Monday morning, April 3, 1865, Mayor Mayo, of Richmond, rode with a committee of citizens about a mile beyond the city limits and there met the Federal troops under the command of Major-General Weitzel, who was marching his army towards the city to take possession. Mayor Mayo requested General Weitzel to occupy the city as quickly as possible, restore order, and protect the women and children. Here you will see a reproduction of a drawing made at the time by an artist of *Leslie's Weekly* showing the first regiment of Federal soldiers to enter Richmond as they marched up Main Street, passing in front of the location occupied for the past *fifty* years by the Everett Waddey Company.

From these ashes was built a modern city, and among the many enterprises established by the men who returned from Lee's army, and who refused to be discouraged, was founded in 1882 a small stationery store and printing plant. From this small beginning the company grew rapidly until today it operates the largest plant of its kind in the entire South, occupying, besides a store on Main Street, an eight-story concrete factory building in the rear that stretches from Eleventh to Twelfth Street, the entire length of the block— a significant change in the path of destruction followed by the Union troops as they marched into Richmond sixty-seven years ago. A high ideal of quality of production, the use of the most modern machinery and intelligent application of industry and forethought are, together with an indulgent and appreciative public, responsible for this achievement.

❧

EVERETT WADDEY COMPANY
Printers ꞏ Lithographers ꞏ Engravers
STATIONERS *and* OFFICE OUTFITTERS

A Sample of Lee's Strategy

Dr. Richard Heath Dabney, of the University of Virginia, Brings This Account of One of the Strategic Masterpieces of World History

THOUGH not in immediate command of any army in the middle of March, 1862, Lee was, as chief military adviser of President Davis, the strategic head of the Confederacy. Magruder, with a force of 11,000, was then holding the lines of Yorktown with the purpose of blocking a hostile advance from Fortress Monroe; Jackson was at Woodstock in the Shenandoah Valley with less than 5,000 men; while Edward Johnson, with not 3,000, was guarding the southern end of the Valley against attack from the west. About 50,000 men lay south of the Rappahannock under Joseph E. Johnston. The Confederate problem, then, was to use these 69,000 Confederates so as to escape destruction by 180,000 Federals and save Richmond from capture. Lee's solution of this knotty problem is one of the strategic masterpieces in the world's history.

When it had finally become clear than McClellan would advance up the Peninsula, Johnston fell back to the vicinity of Richmond, leaving a small body of troops at Fredericksburg and about 8,000 men under Ewell on the upper Rappahannock. Davis now placed Magruder and his force under the command of Johnston, who, after examining Magruder's position and finding

Gen. Robert E. Lee

a good deal of sickness among his troops, advised that Yorktown be evacuated and that the largest obtainable army be concentrated at Richmond with a view to attacking McClellan when he approached.

Johnston was an able general, and much could be said for his plan. But Lee's vision of the whole strategic field was clearer and more comprehensive. Having recently been in charge of the South Atlantic coast, he saw the military and political danger of weakening the defenses of Charleston and Savannah by sending to Richmond the forces which Johnston desired. There were, moreover, other factors in the situation which Lee firmly grasped. Great as was the

danger from McClellan's army, there was also the danger that, when that army moved up from the sea, other formidable forces would converge from other parts of Virginia and, combining with McClellan's army, overwhelm any force which could be brought to the defense of Richmond. What and where were these forces?

Ever since the battle of Bull Run, Lincoln had been tremulous for the safety of Washington. When, therefore, he had permitted McClellan to take the "Army of the Potomac" to Fortress Monroe, he placed McDowell at the head of another army, which was expected both to act as a shield for Washington and to be ready to effect a junction with McClellan when he approached Richmond. This army, which soon contained 30,000 men, and, ere long, 40,000, had, by the middle of April, reached the Rappahannock opposite Fredericksburg. At the same time the lower Shenandoah Valley was occupied by 20,000 under Banks, while Frémont, with 15,000 more in Western Virginia, had already sent part of his force under Milroy toward the upper end of the Valley. Should all of these armies combine with McClellan's, what hope was there for Richmond? Very little indeed. But the far-seeing strategy of Lee devised ways and means of preventing that combination and of assailing McClellan unaided by the other armies. Lee well understood both McClellan and Lincoln, and knew how to play upon the weaknesses of each. If he could stimulate Lincoln's alarm for the safety of his capital, Lincoln might not venture to let McDowell go too far from Washington. But how could he increase Lincoln's alarm? By first alarming Banks, who guarded the fords by which a Confederate army might cross the Potomac and swoop upon Washington. Lee also knew that McClellan was a slow and cautious commander—too

(Continued on page 46)

President Jefferson Davis received by Lee and his Generals before Richmond—An artist's conception

When the Tide Flowed Around the Capital

Col. H. L. Landers, U. S. A., Is One of the Outstanding Authorities on the Seven Days Around Richmond. He Discusses Here the Engagements of That Period, Leaders North and South, and Relates How the Tide of Battle Was Turned

AN AWESOME TIDE, slowly and silently flooding its course with immeasurable force to the last barrier of a nation's capital; an army of youth, valiantly struggling to preserve that citadel which enshrined the spirit of the South; a community that saw the invading shadow lengthen to its very door—such was Richmond, when in the second year of the War Between the States, Fair Oaks and Seven Pines became the barrier against which the hungry tide spent its futile force.

With what feelings did the Government of the Confederacy, the women and children and the old men of Richmond, await the fulfilment of the specter's growth? With such a sublime confidence in government and army as to light the way for other great cities a half century later. With the "utmost confidence in the skill and ability of our General" and the hope that he would "be left free and untrammelled to carry out his own views, and to make his campaign in his own way." When "Close Quarters" and "The Critical Moment" were the captions of the editorials

to calm the inquietude, it was found that within the kingdom of their own souls had fear been conquered.

There is a singular freedom from hysteria noted as one reads the papers of the period. When the belated news of battle passed from mouth to mouth on the streets of Richmond, it had lost the sting of sharp impact. The sorrow of those who mourned loved ones was softened by the all-enveloping thought that a greater thing than human life was endangered—the life of a nation. There was but "little alarm"—"no fear"—"composed calm"—"quiet dignity," and "calm equanimity." Thus it was during the World War that London received the bomber—that Paris carried on despite the long-range artillery.

Seven Pines cost the South, for a time, a gallant leader, but President Davis had by his side a modest, lovable, and loyal soldier into whose keeping he gave the valiant army that said, "Here we stand." From the hands that had won fame and glory in battle did Joe Johnston pass the sword to the hands of Robert E. Lee, who was to grow into

Left: A pontoon bridge thrown across waters near Richmond. Below: Fortifications used in the attack upon the city. Inserts: Joseph E. Johnston, Stonewall Jackson.—(Brady Album)

the Great Soldier of the South—the most Christ-like man in character who ever fought for principle, home and country.

And what a war it was that occupied these giant combatants! The frontier line marked by the border States of Missouri, Kentucky, and Maryland measured 1,100 miles. Where has there even been another of such magnitude? Lee and McClellan became more than leaders of great armies—one the guardian of an infant nation, the other the conservator of a united country. Upon their immediate successes and failures depended the future of all the States. Their battles were more than conflict of arms—they were the deeds upon which rested the foundation of the Confederacy; and by which it was hoped to maintain the integrity of the United States.

Critics who censure McClellan for not marching into Richmond, or Lee for not striking sooner, are superficial. They write from a half-digested analysis of cause and effect, plans and execution. Generally their knowledge of the ground is obtained only from maps and books. Why should they assume judgeship with so little knowledge of nature? Let a man sink into the mire of the Chickahominy and wade White Oak Swamp before he sits in judgment.

McClellan was called the "Dirt Digger" because, by magic, he did not remove the Chickahominy. His army made Herculean efforts to bridge that treacherous stream, but nature fought with unprecedented rainfall to frustrate its efforts. He had to dig to make his army safe for the

moment. And so did Lee. If Lee were to refuse to listen to the clamors of those who averred that military necessity demanded the abandonment of Richmond, he, too, must acquire security by becoming a "Dirt Digger."

You, who were there, did not like this, for the army was too new to appreciate the necessity that soldiers engage in such lowly occupation. But your great leader did not see why he should leave to his adversary "the whole advantage of labour." He knew that "combined with valour, fortitude and boldness, of which we have our fair proportion, it should lead us to success." He told you that it was this humble occupation which "carried the Roman soldiers into all countries."

In time labor ended and war was resumed. That meteor in the Valley, who during these shadowed days was brilliantly executing maneuvers and winning battles which today are studied by military men throughout the world, was called to Richmond to confer with Lee. How magnificently Stonewall Jackson gave his support; how loyally he became the subordinate strong arm of Lee, is knowledge sacredly guarded in the breast of every son and daughter of the South. Their earthly companionship ended soon after Chancellorsville, and how dear to each of them must have been its resumption beyond!

The Confederate Army began the campaign of the Seven Days under the first operations order ever issued by General Lee for a large command. It is unusually complete, and presents in a clear and logical manner the wishes of the commander. It contains but few equivocal matters, and stands today as one of the best orders of the Civil War. Strange to say historians generally have carelessly analyzed it. They are confused as to what was expected of Jackson's Corps at Mechanicsville. They do not understand ground, and blindly assume that Lee intended concentrating the attack of four big corps—those of Longstreet, A. P. Hill, D. H. Hill, and Jackson—on the short front at Beaver Dam Creek. Had Jackson tried to participate in this battle on the 26th of June, he could have reached Fitz John Porter's lines only by walking over the troops of the two Hills.

You, who were there, recall the entrenched position,

(Continued on page 48)

Fredericksburg

The Great Battles Around This City and the Park Area Are Described by Thomas Lomax Hunter

Dementi Photo

House in which General Stonewall Jackson died

FREDERICKSBURG'S position on the south bank of the Rappahannock River, half way between Washington and Richmond, and upon the railroad which links the two capitals, made it the natural storm center of the War Between the States.

Spotsylvania County, in which the City of Fredericksburg is located, saw more of the fighting and had more of the blood of that bitter conflict shed upon its soil than any other county in America. It is named for one of Virginia's most gallant and romantic Colonial figures, Alexander Spottswood. He was born in Tangier, Africa, in 1676, entered the British Army, served on the staff of the Duke of Marlborough at Blenheim and carried the first tidings of that great victory to England. From 1710 to 1722 he was Lieutenant Governor of Virginia, doing much to promote the interest of the colony and leading the first expedition over the Blue Ridge Mountains, over a route now traversed by a splendid highway known as "The Spottswood Trail."

The town of Fredericksburg had its first sight of the armed forces of the Union on the 19th of April, 1862, when General Marsena R. Patrick marched into it and placed it under military rule. It was evacuated in the following August but enjoyed only a brief respite, for on the 10th of the following November Captain Dahlgren's Federal Dragoons rode into the city and a few days later the hosts of Burnside lined the Stafford hills.

The first major engagement which took place in this neighborhood was the Battle of Fredericksburg. After the Confederate repulse at Antietam, McClellan marched his army leisurely into Virginia and reached Warrenton in the

Left: Street scene in Fredericksburg following the bombardment of the city. Above: Group of Confederates inspect a wrecked railroad bridge—
(Brady Album)

early days of November, 1862. To meet this threat, Lee moved with Longstreet's Corps to Culpeper, leaving Jackson in Winchester.

(Continued on page 61)

Washington and Lee University, known as Washington College during the Presidency of Gen. R. E. Lee

The Granary of the Confederacy

Campaigns in the Valley of Virginia, the Race Track of Two Great Armies, Are Described Here by Allen W. Moger

THE rolling country of the Valley of Virginia, flanked by the Blue Ridge on the east and the Alleghanies on the west, drained by the winding Shenandoah, "Daughter of the Stars," and cut by the picturesque Massanutten range which rises out of the plain near Strasburg and ends abruptly within the northern boundary of Rockingham County, not only attracts visitors because of its scenic panorama of beauty and charm, but will ever arouse the interest of those who find delight in historic deeds of the past. This region played a most significant part in the epoch-making struggle between the North and South, for its unusual fertility and wealth and its geographical form and location made its control of material and strategic importance to the armies of the Confederacy.

This "Granary of the Confederacy" had for many years been famous for the production of wheat and other grains. And it is not surprising that in this valley Cyrus H. McCormick invented and perfected his

reaper, which, by a strange irony, through its later use on the prairies of the Mid-West, became one of the most effective weapons employed by the North against Virginia and the South, to which Mr. McCormick always felt warmly attached.

While secession was not popular in the Valley at first, sentiment definitely turned after it was evident that Lincoln intended to use force. The governor of Virginia, John Letcher, who was from that section, opposed secession, but he began to favor it when the President called upon him for Virginia's quota of volunteers. Among those who persisted in their loyalty to the Union are Alexander H. H. Stuart and John B. Baldwin, brothers-in-law in Staunton, and Rev. George Junkin, father-in-law of Stonewall Jackson and a native of Pennsylvania who had served as an able and popular president of Washington College since 1848.

(Continued on page 66)

The Jackson Arch and Statue, Virginia Military Institute

The Capitol of the Confederacy (Va. State Capitol) in war days. Below: President Jefferson Davis (Brady Album)

Richmond: Capital of the Confederacy

The Secession Convention--How Virginia Received the News--Arrival of Jefferson Davis--Weary Years of the War--The Fall of the Capital--The Trail to Appomattox, are Discussed Here by J. Malcolm Bridges

MEMORIES like trooping phantoms pass in review before those who care to turn back to April of 1861. Ships were riding at anchor on the James, flinging from their mastheads the Stars and Stripes of the Union, each a replica of the flag that floated lazily from its staff atop the Jefferson-designed Capitol of Virginia. Perched upon its hill, one of the seven upon which Richmond was builded, the stately old building was in full view of the river and readily observed by the seamen who had brought cargoes to discharge at the port to make room for more precious burdens before turning down stream.

The ships seemed anxious to remain at the doors of Richmond, awaiting they knew not what. On deck the work went on as usual, a jib to be tightened here, a sail to be repaired there. But the seamen, as they finally prepared to leave the port, cast their keen eyes in the direction of the white Capitol upon the hill, noted the flag flung to the April breeze, and discredited somewhat the news that had reached them from the waterfront.

For nearly two months a convention had been in session at the Capitol. The question being deliberated was that of secession. Virginia was exerting every effort, employing every means at her command, to avert the war she deemed inevitable in case of disunion. But it is too late now. On

April 14 news reached Richmond of the fall of Fort Sumter and a hundred guns roared in the city in celebration of the event; impatient citizens who had followed the deliberations of the convention with intense interest crowded the streets, asking one another if the fire of the guns meant that Virginia had joined hands with her sister States of the South. Richmond church bells tolled throughout the night, their musical notes blending somehow with the strains of a new melody—"Dixie"—being played and sung on every street.

But secessionists, doomed to disappointment, must wait until the 17th to receive the news they desired to hear. Upon that date the Secession Convention, meeting within the building made forever sacred by the memories of those who had gone before, unanimously adopted the resolution:

The people of Virginia recognize the American principle, that government is founded on the consent of the governed, and the right of the people of the several States of this Union, for just cause, to withdraw from their association, under the Federal government, with the people of the other States, and to erect new governments for their better security; and they never will consent that the Federal power, which is in part their power, shall be exerted for the purpose of subjecting such States to the Federal authority.

Down was hauled the flag from its lofty perch atop the State Capitol; down came the emblems from the mastheads of the craft riding at anchor or moored to the wharves that formed the very door of Richmond. Replacing the Stars and Stripes was a new design, emblem of a new country, the Stars and Bars of the Confederate States of America.

For days Richmond celebrated the decision of the convention. All business was suspended for the time; rockets

flared by night and lights gleamed from every window; enthusiasm for the cause took the form of hysteria. Orators from other States reached the city, one from Georgia, several from North Carolina, another from Baltimore, who related in some detail how the passage of Federal troops through his city had been resisted.

Although it had been slow to pass the ordinance of secession, the Virginia Convention moved rapidly to prepare for defense. Less than a week passed before the body greeted Col. Robert E. Lee as he appeared to receive his commission as commander of the armed forces of Virginia. John Janney, its chairman, greeted the man of military bearing as he entered the historic hall of the House of Delegates:

"Major-General Lee," he began, "in the name of the people of our native State here represented, I bid you a cordial and heartfelt welcome to this hall in which we may yet hear the echo of the voices of the statesmen and soldiers and sages of bygone days who have borne your name, whose blood now flows in your veins. When the necessity became apparent of having a leader for our forces, all hearts and all eyes, with an instinct which is a surer guide than reason itself, turned to the old County of Westmoreland. . . Yesterday your Mother, Virginia, placed her sword in your hands upon the implied condition that you will draw it only in defense, and that you will fall with it in your hand rather than the object for which it is placed there should fail."

Standing erect, near the speaker's chair, Lee responded: "Profoundly impressed by the solemnity of this occasion, for which I must say I was not prepared, I accept the position assigned me by your partiality. I would have much preferred had the choice fallen upon an abler man. Trusting in Almighty God, an approving conscience and the aid of

my fellow-citizens, I devote myself to the service of my State, in whose behalf alone will I ever again draw my sword."

While Richmond and surrounding country took on the aspect of a great encampment, events in the deeper South were being shaped with the city in mind. It was deemed expedient to remove the seat of the Confederate government from Montgomery, Ala., to Virginia's capital. Richmond was nearer the center of activities, nearer the scenes of the contemplated military movements, and a strategic point of more importance.

Soon thereafter President Jefferson Davis arrived in the city and took up temporary quarters in the old Spotswood Hotel. His room was decorated with the colors of the Confederacy; flags were unfurled from every guestroom. A delegation of Richmond citizens called to offer him a home, which he refused to accept as a gift but agreed to occupy when rented by the government.

They were busy days for Richmond. More officials were arriving each hour. Offices were established for the newly-formed government. The War Department Building was designated. The President's office was furnished and occupied by the grave man from Mississippi. What seemed to be an endless supply of troops arrived and were quartered in or near the city—regiment after regiment, without the necessary uniforms or equipment, grim-faced men who knew what to expect of war, younger men and boys who knew little of its horrors but who would live to learn.

Meanwhile, Richmond women were plying the needle, each a self-appointed seamstress for the soldiers. In the words of a resident of that

(Continued on page 44)

An artist's conception of the evacuation and burning of Richmond, April 2, 1865

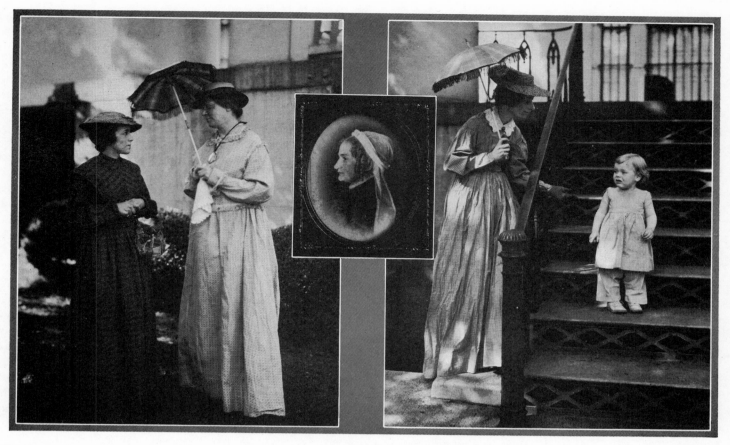

The pictures above were arranged especially for "Richmond" by the Confederate Museum. In the left panel may be seen a homespun dress and hat of the war period, while the light dress is a calico garment for which Mrs. Jefferson Davis paid $1,000. Center: Mrs. Robert E. Lee, wife of General Lee. In the right panel may be seen another costume of the war period and a child's dress worn by an infant who ran the blockade from Georgia to Washington during the war.

The Prop of the Swan's-down Fan

Captain Sally Tompkins, Tillie Russell, Zora Fair and Other Feminine Soldiers of the Confederacy Are Paid High Tribute Here by Miss Mary Maury Fitzgerald

"OH, YES! I'll miss him mightily—but I ain't never cried about his going. I never shed a tear for the old man nor for the boys, neither and I ain't a-goin' ter. Them Yankees must not come a-nigh Richmond; if they does, I'll fight 'em myself."

The speaker was a country woman, who, from the depleted stock of a Richmond shop in 1864, was endeavoring to equip "her old man," too infirm to fight the Yankees, to drive an ambulance. An ambulance driver was not properly of the service in her opinion and hence unentitled to be outfitted by the quartermaster, so that uniform and equipment were made and assembled by the same hands which had sent four sons to join General Lee. Her remarks were addressed to a Virginia lady who expressed her admiration of the woman's sacrifice. "You are certainly a patriot," she said. "Yes, honey," the woman assented, unconscious of the compliment implied, "Ain't you? Ain't everybody?"

This was the attitude of the women of the Confederacy.

No service was shirked, no situation was too difficult; no sacrifice was considered too great. Accustomed to large scale housekeeping and wholesale provisioning, the equipment of an army—from uniforms and leather cartouches to lead for bullets and lint for wounds—was quite a different proposition.

"In half a century woman's place has changed more, probably, than in all her previous history," says a recent writer. We women perhaps should sympathize with ourselves in so difficult a dilemma. Let us not, however, be misled into thinking that womankind has not been in quandaries before and, above all, let us remember how she has met them. Today, woman is being trained as adequately as possible in technical schools and colleges to meet the requirements of her place in a rapidly changing world. The equilibrium which she finds hard to achieve has always been difficult of attainment. Her position has shifted in rhythm with our civilization—an advantage which the

(Continued on page 74)

Defense and Defenders of Hampton Roads

*Clifford Millard, of Norfolk, Who Has Spent Ten Years Studying the Engagements
in This Great Area, Discusses the Battle of the Virginia-Monitor
and Other Important Naval Conflicts*

THE FIRST defensive work in Virginia was built on Jamestown Island in the year 1607. Two years later Capt. John Smith related that Cape Comfort was "a little Isle fit for a Castle," but it was not until 1611 that Algerourne Fort was built there. Its seven guns provided scant protection against a jealous Spanish King whose ships were in constant search for the English settlers. In 1632 a stronger work arose on Old Point Comfort, but was quite useless by 1639. One hundred years later Fort George, built of brick, was erected near the site of the present Chamberlin Hotel.

While the defenses at Jamestown served to protect the colony from the Indians, Fort Henry and Fort Charles on Southampton River were erected about 1610 and served, along with Algerourne, to discourage an attack by Spaniards in the year 1611. Yet the defenses of Hampton Roads were powerless to prevent Dutch men-of-war from sailing past the Point and capturing or destroying English craft

in 1667 and again in 1673. There were no land works on the Chesapeake Bay shore to annoy the pirates who nested near Cape Henry for nearly a century.

The colonists made desultory attempts to fortify Old Point Comfort during the eighteenth century, and Lord Cornwallis inspected the place in 1781. He did not, however, attempt to occupy it.

An English fleet entered Hampton Roads during the War of 1812. The English admiral, failing to capture Norfolk and Portsmouth by firing from his vessels, attempted to land troops for a flanking movement, but the Americans repulsed the attempt in the action of Craney Island. The English then sacked the town of Hampton. This marked the last invasion by a foreign fleet of Hampton Roads.

The construction of Fortress Monroe began in 1819 upon land owned by the Commonwealth of Virginia, and deeded to the Federal Government in 1838. It (Continued on page 70)

Commodore Maury, from an original photo

*"Virginia-Merrimac" attacking the Federal ship,
"Cumberland"*

© Confederate Memoria lInstitute

Maury Memorial, Monument Avenue

*Left: Battery No. 5, the Gun Encamp-
ments. Below: Gracie's Salient and
Gracie's Dam*

Dementi Photos

Petersburg's
Three Hundred Days

*Being a Description by the Distinguished Historian, Dr.
Arthur Kyle Davis, of the Various Engagements
and Final Fall of the City*

[Copyrighted 1932, by Arthur Kyle Davis]

THREE HUNDRED DAYS and the labor and valor of
some 200,000 troops went to the making of the Petersburg battlefield area. The Petersburg National Military
Park contains perhaps the most embattled stretch and the
greatest permanent military work in America. For Petersburg was not only the Waterloo of the Confederacy, but
also its Verdun with a sterner fate.

These hills and fields south of the Appomattox show today
the four lines of entrenchment, little touched by the hand of
time. The fifty permanent forts and hundred batteries are
all centered upon the famous Confederate
Dimmock line, a semi-circle of fifty-five
batteries in ten miles of fortifications around
the city. Just seventy years ago, in the
summer of 1862, this line was built, and
for seven decades nature has had this area
of fighting, this cockpit of the Confederacy, in her kindly care.

THE PETERSBURG LINES: For forty miles, from the
Chickahominy near Richmond, across the James at Deep
Bottom and Drewry's Bluff, and on to the Appomattox at
Battery 1 and Fort McGilvray, and then around Petersburg to Hatcher's Run, stretch the two lines of offense and
defense. But for miles east and south and west of the city,
these two lines became four, two Confederate and two
Federal; for at Fort Fisher began Grant's reverse line of
fortifications, a loop enclosing his ten-mile military railroad
to City Point. The Confederates also had two lines, for
Beauregard was driven from part of the "Dimmock Line"
to the "Siege Line" nearer the city. It was this twenty-mile
stretch of fortifications south of the Appomattox that bore
the brunt of the fighting, for it was here that the fate of the
Confederacy was decided.

This decision was not made in a three-day battle, as at
Gettysburg, the year before the Petersburg siege, nor in
three great battles, as in the Wilderness, Spotsylvania and
Cold Harbor in the month preceding the siege, but in a
long series of battles and assaults from Battery 5 and the
Rives Salient in June of '64 to Hatcher's Run and Five
Forks in April of '65. For ten
months, lacking one week, the eyes
of the world were fixed on Peters-

*Confederate Tunnels, under-
ground cross-roads near Ft.
Mahone*

Right: The front of the Crater of Elliott's Salient.

Below: Rifle pits in advance of Battery No. 5

burg. When the long drama ended and Petersburg fell on April 2, 1865, the surrender at Appomattox a week later was merely an epilogue.

GRANT'S VIRGINIA CAMPAIGNS: Grant waged two campaigns in Virginia and only two, the Richmond campaign and the Petersburg campaign. Both of these were sieges. Swinton says that the Overland campaign for Richmond was "a kind of running siege," but it needs no historian to tell that the Petersburg campaign was "a kind of sitting-down siege." Here Grant sat down first to cut Lee's lines of supplies and later to destroy Lee's army.

In two respects the siege of Petersburg is a study in the newer methods of war. It was a campaign for railways and it was a campaign of trench strategy. It was a ten-month fight for roads and lines of supplies, for the Weldon Railroad the Jerusalem Plank Road to the south and for the Southside Railroad and the Boydton Plank Road to the west. When these lines were cut, Petersburg fell. In this long effort modern trench warfare began, and fifty years later in the World War, as Eckenrode says, "The trench lines on the Aisne and the Marne repeated the trench lines on the Appomattox." In the maze of works and the welter of battles, only a brief outline of ten selected episodes may be given. These episodes include the stories of Battery 5, the Maine Monument, Fort Stedman, Gracie's Salient, the Crater, Rives Salient, the Confederate Tunnels, Fort Gregg, Fort Fisher, and Blandford Church, all of which are pictured in this article and all of which are easily accessible in the order named.

THE TWO THREATS: It was in 1862, two years before Grant's move against the city, that McClellan planned to take Petersburg. After the Seven Days Battles, around Richmond, McClellan had 90,000 troops at

Jerusalem Plank Road, to "Jerusalem" between "Hell" and "Damnation"

Harrison's Landing, and he planned to cross the James, take Petersburg, and cut the Confederate lines of supplies from the south. At first the plan met with favor and Lincoln visited McClellan at his base, but the final decision to withdraw the Federal army from the James-York Peninsula saved Petersburg at that time. In the meantime, however, Lee had seen the danger and he sent Gen. D. H. Hill to fortify the city. Thus it was that the work of defense began here, which grew into the Dimmock line, completed in 1863.

The second threat against Petersburg came from General Butler. In May of 1864, he landed his Army of the James of 30,000 at Bermuda Hundred and City Point and began his advance up the Appomattox-James Peninsula against Petersburg and Richmond. He was checked by Beauregard at Drewry's Bluff on May 16th and was then driven back and corked up, "like a fly in a bottle," as Grant said, by Beauregard's line of entrenchment across the Peninsula at Howlett's Neck. In this advance, however, Butler had sent General Kautz with 2,400 cavalry south of Petersburg

(Continued on page 50)

Objects of Confederate Interest in the Virginia State Library

Dr. H. R. McIlwaine, Virginia State Librarian, Picks Relics and Documents of Special Interest From His Treasure-House in Capitol Square

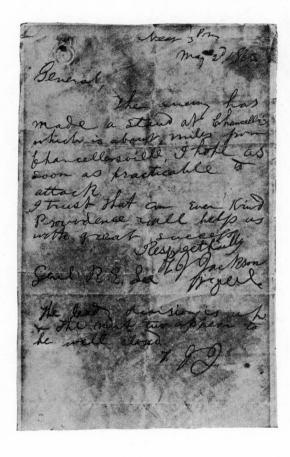

Last dispatch sent by Stonewall Jackson to General Lee, most valuable document in the Library

Sword of Major von Borck who served on staff of Gen. J. E. B. Stuart during war. This sword will be on display at the Confederate Museum during the Reunion

Dementi Photos

ON THE NIGHT of April 2-3, 1865, occurred the greatest tragedy in the history of the City of Richmond. On that night the troops of the Confederacy evacuated the city and detachments of the conquering Union Army marched in the next morning. The magazines containing military stores of all kinds were set on fire by the retiring Confederates and the flames were quickly communicated to adjacent buildings and from them to their neighbors, so that before the fire could be subdued the next day (the Federal soldiers assisting in the work of fighting the flames) the greater part of the business section of the city had been destroyed.

The fire ate its way up to the old State Court building occupying the site of the present State Office building, and the building and its contents were entirely destroyed. The records in that building, early court records of the Colony and the State of Virginia and the court records of several of the counties of Virginia, sent there for safekeeping, were a total loss, a loss which could never be repaired. No Confederate records (that is, records of the Confederate government) were in the building, it is believed. These were in the buildings occupied by the several executive departments of the Confederate government and in the State Capitol, which was used during the time that Richmond was the capital city of the Confederacy as the meeting place of the Confederate Congress. Not a great many Confederate records were lost as a result of the fire, though many of them were undoubtedly stolen in the confusion of the times by relic hunters and others. They were shortly shipped to Washington, where they remain to this day.

Probably the most interesting of them are the pay rolls of the companies from all the Southern States in the service of the Confederacy. When the paymasters in the field paid off the companies and received on the pay rolls the signatures of the men paid off or of their representatives, the pay rolls were sent to Richmond to constitute the vouchers of the paymasters. There were pay rolls (or should have been) of every company in the service, some-

(Continued on page 43)

Federal Raids on the Confederate Capital

Earle Lutz Bring This Story of Thrusts at the Heart of the Old Confederacy, of Alarms, Some Unfounded, Others Serious, Answered by Richmond's Home Guard During the War Between the States

THOSE were thrilling days in Richmond when great masses of Bluecoats battered vainly at her portals. Then the thunders of battle were music to a populace tuned to confidence in the prowess of the unyielding human breastwork barring every road and by-path.

There were other days, however, when the premonitory bell in Capitol Square found only clerks, civilians, convalescents and boys to rally to the defense. Then a chill of dread went through the beleaguered city as the swift hoofbeats of invading cavalry drowned out the unmartial tread of the volunteers rushing to the posts of danger.

But just as the Confederate regulars made glorious records for valor on the bloody fields of Seven Pines, Cold Harbor and Malvern Hill, so the ill-sorted defenders of the capital were never found wanting, even when the swift swoops of Stoneman, Kilpatrick and Sheridan brought the enemy within the outer circle of defending breastworks. Just as suffering and distress inspired the people to the sweetest and noblest actions of which they were capable, so did the necessity for preservation of home and fireside imbue old and young with bravery and courage to resist every thrust at the heart of the Confederacy.

And while some of the alarms answered by Richmond's home guard verged on the ridiculous, yet others were of the most serious nature and with a trifle more boldness might have resulted in the capture of America's Verdun. Chiefly the raids were quixotic in conception and had no military results of importance.

Richmond's earliest alarm provided the city with many a laugh—when it was over. It was in the gala days of the war, in fact, before bloody Manassas made the capital one big hospital. It came on a bright Sunday morning in April of '61. As the congregations came pouring out of the churches, the tocsin in the Square clanged its warning. Men rushed to their armories and in record time the militia companies had mustered and were hastening down the river to repel the Federal sloop of war, *Pawnee*, which was reported steaming up the James to destroy Richmond. Artillery was posted, but the first movement of Virginia's military forces was needless as the report was unfounded and the soldiery returned home with sheepish grins.

For a long period, Richmonders were concerned with the possibility of attack from the water. But the feats of the ironclad *Merrimac*, re-christened *Virginia*, allayed the terror from this source for a time and then the ability of the defenses at Drewry's Bluff became unquestioned. This test came on May 15, 1862, when an enemy fleet of five ships of war made a sudden dash up the James, bent on reaching the capital. Leading the invading flotilla were the *Monitor* and the *Galena*. A panic was imminent in the city, but soon the people breathed freer with the news that the dreaded foe had been checked. The report was true. The *Galena* and *Monitor* came within 600 yards of the forts and opened fire. Shore batteries rained shell into the invaders. After two hours the enemy drew off, realizing that it was almost impossible to challenge the river defenses.

For the first two years of the war, Richmond saw all attacks pushed aside and a kaleidoscopic change in Federal commanders as a result of their inability to take the Southern stronghold.

(Continued on page 58)

The Confederate Tradition of Richmond

Dr. Douglas S. Freeman, Editor of the Richmond News Leader, reminds us here that the War Between the States made Richmond a symbol, the center of a great tradition bound up with a long defence

RICHMOND was a name in 1860; the War Between the States made her a symbol. She had been the home of a few great men; she became the center of a great tradition. Her ways had been the ways of pleasantness; her fame is that of war. With Leyden and Londonberry her stout defence won her a place in history; the success of that defence took on the same moral significance that led men to regard the tricolor on the citadel of Verdun as the symbol of allied victory or defeat in 1916. As long as Richmond defied the foe, the Southern Confederacy never lost hope. When Richmond fell, the Southern cause collapsed.

Strategically it probably was a mistake to move the capital of the Confederate States from Montgomery in May, 1861, and to place it within a hundred miles of the frontier. It was done to recognize the value to the Confederacy of the adhesion of Virginia and to rally the border States to secession; but it would have been better if President Davis, like Frederick the Great, had fixed his capital wherever the course of conflict carried his standard. Had this been done, each of the tidal rivers of the South Atlantic seaboard might in turn have covered the battle-line, as the Tagliamento and the Piave did for Italy after Caporetto, or as the Meuse, the Aisne and the Marne did for France in 1914. The vigor of the Union offensive might then have been exhausted as the lines of communication were lengthened, and the end might perhaps have been different.

But the decision was made. Congress and the executives moved to Richmond. The Tredegar became the Krupp Works of the Confederacy, and by the spring of 1862, when the first echo of McClellan's guns came in an ominous mutter of hate from the Chickahominy, Richmond already meant so much to the Confederacy that the evacuation of the city, though seriously considered, would have been regarded alike in the North and in the South as the preliminary of ruin. The great battles of 1862 and 1863 made the successful defence of Richmond the great object of Confederate strategy, even to the neglect of Vicksburg and the line of the Tennessee River. The Confederacy was reft in twain because the pride of the Administration made it hold Richmond at any price and to construct here the munition works that should have been placed far to the interior. Even in the autumn of 1864, when the uncomplaining Lee confessed that Richmond had become a millstone around the neck of the Confederacy, the government was unwilling to face the loss of prestige that would follow the abandonment of the city. When Richmond was at last evacuated, it was too late.

Richmond's greatest Confederate tradition, therefore, is bound up with her long defence against an enemy that was immeasurably superior in man-power and in all the *matériel* of war. No narrative that measures the odds against the South simply by the size of the opposing armies tells half the story. Artillery for field-use and for the fortifications had to be captured, imported through an ever-stiffening

blockade or manufactured at improvised plants. Virtually all the guns that guarded the rivers of Virginia and Carolina came from the Gosport Navy Yard, which Virginia seized immediately after she seceded. The small-arms machinery that was used at the Richmond arsenal was brought, in the main, with infinite labor and unregarding haste from Harper's Ferry. There was the direst shortage of powder until the summer of 1862. Harness was almost unprocurable. Hundreds of the horses that hauled the field artillery at Gettysburg were hitched with ragged rope. Not a blanket could be manufactured in the South after the burning of the Crenshaw plant in Richmond. The supply of draught animals was so scant that the Army of Northern Virginia was threatened with immobility by the autumn of 1863. Locomotives could not be replaced. When the military railroad from Danville to Greensboro was constructed, many of the rails used on it came from other lines that had to be wrecked to supply them. The South had never produced as much bacon as it consumed, and after eighteen months of fighting, was forced to reduce the daily ration in the principal armies to four ounces of bacon, with a pint of meal. A hundred instances of like military disadvantages might be cited. All of them contribute to the picture of a people forced to extemporize every essential element of defense and to rely on valor and generalship to resist the odds against them. Rarely was a major battle fought in Virginia that did not find the Confederates hungry on the field of victory and unable, through the exhaustion of the horses and the breakdown of wagons, to pursue the defeated foe. To understand Richmond's place in Confederate tradition, one must try to recreate not only the army in the field, but the engineers busily directing the servants in throwing up the fortifications of the city, and, behind them, thousands of men and women ceaselessly employing the crudest tools to provide the essentials of war, with defeat certain for the army if the machines broke down or the creaking trains ceased running. It is a tradition of hard work not less than of gallant deeds, a tradition of mechanical ingenuity not less than of military strategy.

Yet it will never be possible to have these undramatic elements in the Confederate background appraised at their rightful valuation. The eyes of posterity will follow the battle flags. The name of Richmond will conjure up the confused pageant of dusty soldiers hurrying through crowded streets, of white-faced men and women standing on the edge of Shockoe Hill and watching the red flash of

RUINS OF CONFEDERATE WAR DEPARTMENT 1865
THE BELLHOUSE FROM WHICH FIRE ALARMS AND TOCSINS WERE RUNG.
THE STANDING MASS WAS CORNER OF ADJUTANT GENERAL COOPER'S OFFICE.

the far-off guns at Cold Harbor—a pageant of hurried couriers bringing the news of victory, of ambulance trains rolling slowly down Broad Street or creeping into the station, of the Virginia Central at Seventeenth and Broad to unload hundreds of powder-grimed, pale-lipped wounded, still dazed by the roar of battle. Richmond will mean the slow music of the dead march as Jackson's body is borne through the town. It will mean the rumble of caissons on the back streets, gas lights at midnight from the gray house at Twelfth and Clay when the president sat in doubtful council; it will mean the arrival of the "flag-of-truce boat" when frenzied mothers rushed the lines of returned prisoners in the Capitol Square to see if the sons who were reported "missing" at Gettysburg had by miracle of mercy escaped the death-hail at the stone wall on Cemetery Ridge. "Starvation parties" where soldiers danced till morning with cotton-frocked beauties and then went back to barracks with only the memory of a smile; St. Paul's Church full of gray coats and women in black, bowing together as Dr. Minnegerode prayed; weddings with tears; gentlewomen keeping vigil by the beds of unknown, dying boys in Richmond's thirty-five hospitals; long rows of upturned red clay at Hollywood, where scores of dead were interred every night with only a penciled shingle to mark the soldier's grave; band music and muffled drums; prayer and profiteering; stalls with second-hand finery that impoverished families had sacrificed; empty markets and high prices; crowded prisons and furtive spies; gnawing want and angry bread riots; threatened raids and the tocsin sounded nervously from the belltower in the Capitol Square; gambling houses and crowded bar rooms; strutting staff officers and crippled heroes; thronged streets and overflowing homes; anxious refugees and pompous Congressmen; brave hearts fired to desperate adventure; high confidence slowly turned to doubt in the winter of 1864-65; whispers of disaster that passed unchallenged; the hurried packing of archives and the quick departure of trains for Danville; the sullen withdrawal of the garrison; the explosion of the magazines, and the burning of the bridges; and then the funeral pyre of Southern hope lighted in the tobacco warehouses—that will always remain the Confederate tradition of Richmond.

It is not, however, the confused tradition of massmovement alone. On the contrary, the history of those terrible years gets its color and its romance from personalities.

(Continued on page 43)

The Richmond

The Fields Described Here by H. J. Eckenrode, Historian for the State Conservation and Development Commission, Ran Red With the Blood of Two Great Armies, the One Striving to Defend, the Other Endeavoring to Take the Capital of the Confederacy

FOR TWO periods in the War Between the States fierce and critical fighting took place in the immediate neighborhood of Richmond. In May-June, 1862, McClellan, in the Peninsular Campaign, came close to Richmond, only to be hurled back from the city in the spectacular Seven Days' Battles, June-July, 1862. Just two years passed and, in May-June, 1864, the same terrain witnessed the struggle between Lee and Grant that culminated at Cold Harbor, on June 3, Richmond was saved, and Grant was forced to lay siege to Petersburg in order to take the capital of the Confederacy.

The Richmond Battlefield Parks will cover the main points in these two struggles, as well as the Richmond-Petersburg siege that lasted from June, 1864, until April, 1865. The State Highway Commission has constructed an excellent scenic road through the battlefield area by means of which travelers are able to reach all points of interest within a comparatively short time and without fatigue.

Travelers, following this route, should pass over the Richmond-Tappahannock Highway, which leads northeast from Richmond, as far as the village of Mechanicsville, five miles out. There the Battlefield Park route proper begins. Mechanicsville itself witnessed the beginning of

Lee's offensive against McClellan, June 26, 1862; and the traveler, turning southeast there, follows the road used by the Confederates in approaching Beaver Dam Creek in the afternoon of that fateful day. Of the battlefield at Beaver Dam Creek, where the Confederates were repulsed, the park owns a part of the Union position.

Going on from Beaver Dam Creek, the traveler follows the line of Fitz-John Porter as the Union corps general withdrew to a new position a mile beyond Gaines' Mill. At the latter place, the site of which is marked, the following Confederates came in contact with the retreating Unionists in the morning of June 27, 1862. The fight that began there ended in the great battle of Gaines' Mill, on Boatswain Creek, in the afternoon of the same day.

This was one of the most critical battles of American history. Lee's men clambered down the slope, through Boatswain Creek, and up the hillside held by Porter's entrenched troops with a gallantry never surpassed; but they were met with equal gallantry and hurled back. Evening approached, and Lee grew anxious. Then it was that Stonewall Jackson attacked from the north while A. P. Hill and Longstreet renewed their assaults. The Union position at the Watt House and beyond was captured, and Porter's corps retreated across the Chicka-

Battlefield Parks

The Sites Were Preserved by a Group of Richmond Citizens and Turned Over to the Commonwealth of Virginia for Further Development. When Fully Completed, the Area Will Be One of the Most Interesting and Best Preserved Military Parks in the World

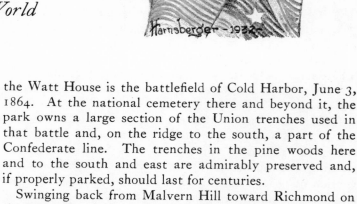

hominy to the main army on the south side of the river. A portion of this battlefield is in the park, including the whole western section and the Watt House, Porter's headquarters. Overhanging Boatswain Creek, this sector will make a beautiful park.

June 29 found Lee in hot pursuit. At Savage's Station, on the Williamsburg Road, Magruder attacked the retiring Unionists but was held off. That night the retreating McClellan hastened across White Oak Swamp. The next day, Lee attacked the Unionists at Glendale, where several roads from Richmond meet; but Jackson was held back by White Oak Swamp, and other bodies of troops failed to get into the battle. The result of one of the most savage fights of the war was that the Union Army continued its retirement to Malvern Hill overlooking the James River.

At Malvern Hill, in the afternoon of July 1, 1862, Lee made his final attack on McClellan. The rough ground made it difficult for the Confederates to bring up artillery and dress their lines, with the result that they were repulsed in a most bitter and bloody battle. The Crew House, Porter's headquarters, and a part of the battlefield belong to the park.

On the battlefield highway a little beyond the turn-in to

the Watt House is the battlefield of Cold Harbor, June 3, 1864. At the national cemetery there and beyond it, the park owns a large section of the Union trenches used in that battle and, on the ridge to the south, a part of the Confederate line. The trenches in the pine woods here and to the south and east are admirably preserved and, if properly parked, should last for centuries.

Swinging back from Malvern Hill toward Richmond on the River Road, the traveler comes to the turn-in to Fort Harrison, for the battlefield route here leaves a main highway. Fort Harrison was an important link in the defenses of Richmond in 1864. Captured in a surprise attack, on September 29, 1864, the fort did not reward the Unionists for their trouble, for beyond it were other defenses just as strong. The park includes miles of fortifications here, almost as good as when built. At Frayser's Farm, the exercises attending the dedication of the park will take place on June 22, 1932. This promises to be one of the most impressive historical ceremonies ever to take place in Virginia. The earthworks are almost perfectly preserved in the woods—a picturesque memorial of the days of long ago.

(Continued on page 60)

Dementi Photos

A Tourist's Guide to Richmond

Where to Go and What to See in the Capital of the Confederate States of America

RICHMOND has retained in her sacred shrines the atmosphere of a by-gone day, each serving to attract thousands of visitors to the city. Many of them house priceless collections of documents and mementos, while others serve as pleasant and at times painful reminders of the early life of a town that was founded when America was young.

It is to the Virginia State Capitol, the structure that served the Confederate States of America for four tragic years, that the visitor turns first. This Jefferson-designed building was the seat of Virginia's historic Secession Convention of 1861. Here General Lee was handed his commission as commander of the armed forces of the Commonweatlh, and here the body of Stonewall Jackson lay in state following the tragedy at Chancellorsville.

While in Capitol Square visitors should view the Confederate memorials; the Crawford equestrian statue of Washington, at the base of which Jefferson Davis was inaugurated as President of the "Permanent Government;" and pause long enough to inspect, however hurriedly, the priceless collection housed in the Virginia State Library.

At the southwest corner of Franklin and Ninth Streets, overlooking Capitol Square, may be seen ST. PAUL'S CHURCH, where Davis and Lee and others high in political and military circles of the Confederacy worshipped while in Richmond. It was while attending services in this church that President Davis was advised of the fall of Petersburg, the dreaded news that resulted in the evacuation of Richmond.

Leaving St. Paul's Church and proceeding north on Ninth Street to Clay and thence east two blocks, the visitor will find the WHITE HOUSE OF THE CONFEDERACY and its invaluable collection of Confederate relics. A room has been set aside in this building as a memorial to each of the Confederate States and from every section of the Old Confederacy has been assembled battle flags, pictures, documents and relics of the war. The White House of the Confederacy is in the care of the Confederate Memorial Literary Society.

One block west, at Eleventh and Clay Streets, is the VALENTINE MUSEUM, with its original model of the recumbent statue of Lee, its books, paintings, prints, and its collection of Virginia and North Carolina archaeology.

Space does not permit of a complete description of the numerous shrines of the city, but for the convenience of the visitors the following brief directory has been compiled:

JOHN MARSHALL HOUSE, Ninth and Marshall Streets. This home was purchased by Chief Justice Marshall in 1795 and occupied by him until 1835. It is now in the care of the Association for the Preservation of Virginia Antiquities, which has gathered and has on display many relics associated with the life of Marshall.

LEE HOME, 707 East Franklin Street. This home was occupied by the Confederate Commander-in-Chief during the short time that he spent in Richmond. Here his family resided and to this house Lee turned following the surrender at Appomattox.

Upper: The Virginia State Capitol.
Lower: The White House of the Confederacy

Edgar Allan Poe Home, Fifth and Main Streets. A tablet in the walls of the building designates this as the site of Poe's early home. The "Literary Messenger" was printed in the building that formerly stood at Fifteenth and Main Streets.

Captain Sallie Tompkins' Hospital, Third and Main Streets. Captain Tompkins, C. S. A., established and operated this hospital at her own expense during three years of the War Between the States, refusing a salary. She is said to be the only woman who held a regular commission in either army.

Gamble's Hill Park, south end of Third and Fourth Streets. Affords an excellent view of the upper river. The hill crest is marked by a cross, as within sight of it is the spot upon which Captain John Smith stood when claiming the territory for England, and designating the section "None Such." Pratt's Castle at the end of Fourth Street was built by an old sea captain. Its architecture is unique, but since it is privately owned, visitors are seldom admitted. Belle Isle, Confederate Prison site, can be seen from the park, as can the Tredegar arsenal of 1861-65.

Where J. E. B. Stuart Died, 210 West Grace Street. The picturesque cavalry leader died here the day following his wounding at Yellow Tavern, in May, 1864.

Monroe Park, Franklin and Main Streets, between Belvidere and Laurel. A fair and camping ground of olden days; now a well-kept square ornamented by several monuments. This was Camp Lee of Confederate fame.

Franklin west of Lombardy Street, in the center of which stands the equestrian statue of Gen. J. E. B. Stuart, is known as Monument Avenue, taking its name from the several handsome monuments located at Lombardy and to the west. The most magnificent residences within the city are to be found on Monument Avenue, along the middle of which extend broad grass plots ornamented at frequent intervals by beds of vari-colored flowers. This is considered one of the most beautiful streets in America. Its monuments, in order, are: Stuart, Lee, Redoubt No. 10 (marking Richmond's inner defenses), Jefferson Davis, Jackson, and Maury.

The Boulevard crosses Monument Avenue, the intersection being marked by the Jackson Monument. The Boulevard, planned similarly to Monument Avenue, takes but slightly lower rank, from the standpoints of beauty and magnificent residences, to the former street, and upon it as one goes south will be found:

The Battle Abbey, or Confederate Memorial Institute, where will be found paintings and murals of great beauty and value. The John Barton Payne collection of rare paintings, a gift to the State of Virginia, is housed in this building. The landscape gardening in the rear of the grounds is as handsome as any in this country.

The Confederate Soldiers' Home is close by and its museum contains many relics of interest. At the southern end of the avenue will be found the West End public athletic field and William Byrd Park, through which the municipal swimming pool may be reached. Just beyond is the new Westover Hills Bridge. Near the east end of the swimming pool is a road leading to Maymont.

Hollywood Cemetery. While in the West End, the visitor should not fail to visit Hollywood Cemetery. Presidents Monroe and Tyler are buried there; also, President Davis and his family, and numerous Virginia governors and heroes, among them being Governor William Smith, General Fitzhugh Lee, General Pickett, General Pegram, General Stuart, John Randolph, of Roanoke, and Commodore Matthew Fontaine Maury. The gigantic pyramid marking the graves of 18,000 Confederate soldiers is ninety feet high. Hollywood, "the burial place of Virginia's dead," is located at the foot of Cherry Street.

Jefferson Park is just to the left of the eastern end, and from here an excellent view of the city may be obtained. One block south is Broad Street, at the extreme eastern end of which is Chimborazo Park, on which was located one of the largest hospitals of the War Between the States. The Weather Bureau is here, and the park overlooks the "Port of Richmond."

Libby Hill Park. This park also affords an excellent view of the city and overlooks (Continued on page 56)

Jefferson Davis Memorial, Monument and Davis Avenues

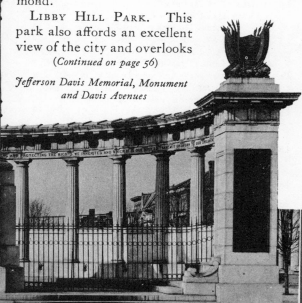

Official Program

Forty-Second Confederate Reunion

WEDNESDAY, JUNE 22
MORNING SESSION
[At the Mosque]

10:00 MUSIC:
Charlottesville Municipal Band.
CONVENTION CALLED TO ORDER:
Gen. Wm. McK. Evans, Commander, Virginia Division, U. C. V.
INVOCATION:
Rev. Thomas K. Gorman, Chaplain General, U. C. V.
PRESENTATION OF GENERAL W. B. FREEMAN, HONORARY COMMANDER FOR LIFE,
Gen. Wm. McK. Evans, Commander, Virginia Division, U. C. V.
SOLO:
Mrs. Emma G. Bell.
WELCOME TO VIRGINIA:
His Excellency, Hon. John Garland Pollard, Governor of Virginia.
RESPONSE:
Dr. H. W. Battle, Charlottesville, Va.
WELCOME TO RICHMOND:
Hon. J. Fulmer Bright, Mayor, City of Richmond.
RESPONSE:
Hon. Geo. H. Armistead, Editor of the *Nashville Banner.*
SPECIAL NUMBERS:
Capitol Choral Club.
ADDRESS:
Gen. C. A. DeSaussure, Commander-in-Chief, U. C. V.
INTRODUCTION OF GEN. HOMER ATKINSON, COMMANDER, ARMY OF NORTHERN VIRGINIA:
Maj. Gen. James Dinkins, Chief of Cavalry, U. C. V.
INTRODUCTION OF GEN. SIMS LATTA, COMMANDER ARMY OF TENNESSEE:
Maj. Gen. James Dinkins, Chief of Cavalry, U. C. V.
INTRODUCTION OF GEN. R. D. CHAPMAN, COMMANDER, TRANS-MISSISSIPPI DEPARTMENT:
Maj. Gen. James Dinkins, Chief of Cavalry, U. C. V.
INTRODUCTION OF GEN. HARRY RENE LEE, ADJUTANT GENERAL AND CHIEF OF STAFF, U. C. V.:
Brig. Gen. J. Colton Lynes, Inspector General, U. C. V.
INTRODUCTION OF MRS. W. B. KERNAN, ASSISTANT TO ADJUTANT GENERAL, U. C. V.
Gen. Harry Rene Lee.
INTRODUCTION OF MISS JESSICA RANDOLPH SMITH, COLOR BEARER, U. C. V.
Gen. Harry Rene Lee.
INTRODUCTION OF GEN. M. D. VANCE, HONORARY COMMANDER FOR LIFE, U. C. V.:
Col. E. N. Yarborough, Confederate Home, Columbia, S. C.
INTRODUCTION OF GEN. R. A. SNEED, HONORARY COMMANDER FOR LIFE, U. C. V.:
Col. W. C. Heath, Monroe, N. C.
INTRODUCTION OF GEN. L. W. STEPHENS, HONORARY COMMANDER FOR LIFE, U. C. V.:
Col. Frank J. Trapp, Assistant Paymaster General, U. C. V.
INTRODUCTION OF REV. GILES B. COOKE, HONORARY CHAPLAIN GENERAL FOR LIFE, U. C. V.:
Mrs. L. M. Bashinsky, Past President General, U. D. C.

INTRODUCTION OF MRS. A. McD. WILSON, PRESIDENT GENERAL, C. S. M. A.:
Brig. Gen. R. E. Bullington, Assistant Adjutant General, U. C. V.
INTRODUCTION OF MRS. W. E. R. BYRNE, PRESIDENT GENERAL, U. D. C.:
Maj. Gen. Wm. Harden, Commander, Georgia Division, U. C. V.
INTRODUCTION OF MISS EDITH POPE, *Confederate Veteran:*
Gen. R. D. Chapman, Commander, Trans-Mississippi Department.
INTRODUCTION OF DR. GEORGE R. TABOR, COMMANDER-IN-CHIEF, S. C. V.:
Brig. Gen. Chas. P. Jones, Chief of Artillery, U. C. V.
SOLO:
Mr. Claude Woodward.
APPOINTMENTS OF COMMITTEE ON CREDENTIALS.
REPORT OF ADJUTANT GENERAL ON CAMPS PAID.
APPOINTMENTS OF COMMITTEE ON RESOLUTIONS.
REPORT OF COMMITTEE ON FINANCE.
UNFINISHED BUSINESS.
NEW BUSINESS.
GENERAL ANNOUNCEMENTS:
Maj. Robert T. Barton, Jr., Chairman, Forty-second Reunion.
BENEDICTION:
Rev. Beverley D. Tucker, Jr., Rector, St. Paul's Episcopal Church.

AFTERNOON SESSION

2:30 FORMAL DEDICATION OF RICHMOND BATTLEFIELD PARKS:
Music by Little Rock High School Band.
8:00 RECEPTION IN HONOR OF THE UNITED CONFEDERATE VETERANS, THE CONFEDERATED SOUTHERN MEMORIAL ASSOCIATION AND THE SONS OF CONFEDERATE VETERANS AT THE MOSQUE AUDITORIUM:
Music by Mississippi State Teachers College Band.
OPENING BALL IN HONOR OF OFFICIAL GUESTS OF THE REUNION:
Admittance by badge or card only, at the Blues' Armory. Music by Augusta Police Band Dance Orchestra.

THURSDAY, JUNE 23
MORNING SESSION
[At the Mosque]

10:00 MUSIC:
Mississippi State Teachers College Band.
CONVENTION CALLED TO ORDER:
Gen. C. A. DeSaussure, Commander-in-Chief, U. C. V.
INVOCATION:
Rabbi E. N. Calisch of the Beth Ahaba Synagogue.
SPECIAL ENTERTAINMENT:
Old Time Fiddlers.

REPORT ON SPECIAL COMMITTEES.
MUSIC:
"That Quartette."
BENEDICTION:
Rev. Giles B. Cooke, Honorary Chaplain General for Life,
U. C. V.

AFTERNOON SESSION

2:30 MUSIC: CLARKSVILLE BOYS BAND.
INVOCATION:
Father L. A. Rowen.
REPORT OF CREDENTIALS COMMITTEE.
REPORT OF COMMITTEE ON RESOLUTIONS.
UNFINISHED BUSINESS.
SOLO:
Mr. Joseph Whittemore.
SELECTION OF REUNION CITY FOR 1933.
ELECTION OF OFFICERS.
MISCELLANEOUS BUSINESS.
SPECIAL NUMBERS:
Acca Temple Chanters.
PRAYER:
Rev. Emmett W. McCorkle, Assistant Chaplain General,
U. C. V.
BENEDICTION:
Rev. Thomas K. Gorman, Chaplain General, U. C. V.

EVENING

9:00 U. C. V. GRAND BALL AT THE GRAYS' ARMORY:
Music by American Legion Band Orchestra.
9:30 BALL IN THE BLUES' ARMORY.
Music by Mississippi State Teachers College Band. Due to
both armories being very small, this other ball will take
care of the overflow crowd at the Grays' Armory. Admission will be by badge or card only.

FRIDAY, JUNE 24
MORNING SESSION

10:30 ALL CONFEDERATE VETERANS ARE REQUESTED TO
REPORT TO THEIR BRIGADES AND DIVISION
COMMANDERS AT THE SOLDIERS' HOME TO BE
ASSIGNED PLACES FOR THE PARADE.
12:00 GRAND PARADE.

EVENING

9:00 S. C. V. GRAND BALL AT THE GRAYS' ARMORY:
Music by local orchestra. Admission by badge or card only.
Members of the United Confederate Veterans and Confederated Southern Memorial Association are invited to
remain for this notable event.

Official Program
*Thirty-third Convention, Confederated Southern
Memorial Association, Richmond, Virginia
June 21-2-3-4, 1932*

MOTTO:
*"Lord God of Hosts, be with us yet,
Lest we forget, lest we forget."*

GENERAL INFORMATION

All meetings of the C. S. M. A. held in the Auditorium of
the Jefferson Hotel.

Luncheon served at Second Baptist Church, Adams and
Franklin Streets, to the Officers, Delegates of the C. S. M. A.
and Invited Guests, courtesy of the Reunion Committee,
Wednesday and Thursday.

Confederate Museum, Twelfth and Clay Streets, and the
Confederate Memorial Institute (Battle Abbey), Kensing-
ton Avenue and Boulevard, open to all Confederate
Organizations during the Reunion.

Thursday, June 23, 1932, at 4:00 p.m., presentation of
the Anchor of the *Virginia-Merrimac* to the Confederate
Memorial Literary Society.

TUESDAY, JUNE 21
[The Jefferson Hotel]
MORNING SESSION

10:00 CONFERENCE OF OFFICERS AND STATE PRESIDENTS
OF THE C. S. M. A.
1:00 LUNCHEON:
John Marshall Hotel, to Mrs. A. McD. Wilson, President
General; Officers and State Presidents, Local Presidents,
C. S. M. A.

AFTERNOON SESSION
[The Jefferson Auditorium]

3:30 MUSIC:
Charlottesville Municipal Band.
MEETING CALLED TO ORDER:
Mrs. John F. Bauer.
INVOCATION:
Reverend Giles B. Cooke.
"DIXIE:"
Charlottesville Municipal Band.
ADDRESS OF WELCOME ON BEHALF OF THE STATE:
Lieut.-Gov. James H. Price.
ADDRESS OF WELCOME ON BEHALF OF THE CITY.
ADDRESS OF WELCOME:
Mrs. B. A. Blenner, State President, C. S. M. A.
GREETINGS:
Gen. C. A. DeSaussure, Commander-in-Chief, U. C. V.
GREETINGS:
Dr. Geo. R. Tabor, Commander-in-Chief, S. C. V.
GREETINGS:
His Excellency Richard B. Russell, Governor of Georgia.
MUSIC:
Charlottesville Municipal Band.
GREETINGS:
Mrs. Charles B. Keesee, State Regent, D. A. R.
GREETINGS:
Mrs. W. E. R. Byrne, President General, U. D. C.
INTRODUCTION OF MRS. A. McD. WILSON, PRESI-
DENT GENERAL, C. S. M. A.
PRESENTATION OF DISTINGUISHED GUESTS.
PRESENTATION OF OFFICIAL LADIES.
ANNOUNCEMENT OF RESOLUTION AND CREDENTIAL
COMMITTEES.
5:00 to 7:00 CONFEDERATED SOUTHERN MEMORIAL ASSO-
CIATION:
Tea at Hillcrest. Invitation by card.
Courtesy of Confederate Memorial Literary Society.
8:00 OPENING MEETING OF THE SONS OF CONFEDERATE
VETERANS HONORING THE UNITED CONFED-
ERATE VETERANS, OFFICIAL LADIES AND MEM-
BERS OF THE CONFEDERATED SOUTHERN MEMO-
RIAL ASSOCIATION.

WEDNESDAY, JUNE 22
[The Jefferson Auditorium]
MORNING SESSION

9:30 CONVENTION CALLED TO ORDER:
Mrs. A. McD. Wilson, President General, C. S. M. A.
INVOCATION:
Rev. Hugh W. Sublett.
MUSIC:
Mississippi State Teachers College Band.
PRESENTATION OF OFFICERS:
Mrs. A. McD. Wilson, President General, C. S. M. A.

REPORT OF CREDENTIALS COMMITTEE.
REPORT OF OFFICERS.
REPORT OF PRESIDENT GENERAL.
REPORT OF RECORDING SECRETARY GENERAL.
REPORT OF CORRESPONDING SECRETARY GENERAL.
REPORT OF AUDITOR GENERAL.
REPORT OF TREASURER GENERAL.
REPORT OF POET LAUREATE GENERAL.
REPORT OF HISTORIAN GENERAL.
REPORT OF NATIONAL ORGANIZER.
REPORT OF STATE PRESIDENTS.
ADJOURNMENT.

———

AFTERNOON

1:00 LUNCHEON TO DELEGATES OF C. S. M. A. AND
INVITED GUESTS, SECOND BAPTIST CHURCH.
2:30 DEDICATION OF RICHMOND BATTLEFIELD PARKS.
(Leaving Richmond at 2:30 p.m.)
8:00 AN EVENING OF THE OLD SOUTH:
Mrs. Bryan Wells Collier, Historian General, C. S. M. A., at
the Mosque Auditorium.
RECEPTION IN HONOR OF THE UNITED CONFEDERATE
VETERANS, THE CONFEDERATED SOUTHERN
MEMORIAL ASSOCIATION AND THE SONS OF
CONFEDERATE VETERANS AT THE MOSQUE
AUDITORIUM.
OPENING BALL IN HONOR OF OFFICIAL GUESTS OF
THE REUNION.
Admittance by badge or card only, at the Blues' Armory.
Music by Augusta Police Band Dance Orchestra.

———

THURSDAY, JUNE 23
[*The Jefferson Auditorium*]
MORNING SESSION

9:30 CONVENTION CALLED TO ORDER:
Mrs. A. McD. Wilson, President General, C. S. M. A.
INVOCATION:
REPORT OF STANDING COMMITTEES.
REPORT OF SPECIAL COMMITTEES.
REPORT OF ASSOCIATIONS. (Limited to five minutes.)

———

[*At the Mosque*]
12:00 MEMORIAL HOUR:
[Convention will suspend business to attend the Memorial Hour
Service of the United Confederate Veterans, Confederated Southern
Memorial Association and Sons of Confederate Veterans to be held
at the Mosque.] Order of exercises arranged by Mrs. A. McD.
Wilson, President General, C. S. M. A.

PROGRAM
ASSEMBLY CALL:
Bugler.
INVOCATION:
Rt. Rev. H. St. G. Tucker, D.D.
HYMN:
"How Firm a Foundation."
ROLL CALL U. C. V.:
Gen. Harry Rene Lee, Adjutant General and Chief of Staff.
ROLL CALL C. S. M. A.:
Miss Daisy M. L. Hodgson, Recording Secretary General,
C. S. M. A.
ROLL CALL S. C. V.:
Walter L. Hopkins, Adjutant-in-Chief, S. C. V.
POEM:
Mrs. Virginia Frazer Boyle, Poet Laureate, U. C. V., C. S.
M. A., S. C. V.
SOLO.
MEMORIAL ADDRESS:
Hon. Hill Montague.
HYMN:
"God Be With You Till We Meet Again."
BENEDICTION:
Rt. Rev. H. St. G. Tucker, D.D.
TAPS.
Miss Audrey Murray, Organist

[*At the Second Baptist Church*]
1:30 LUNCHEON TO DELEGATES OF THE C. S. M. A. AND
INVITED GUESTS.

———

[*At the Jefferson Auditorium*]
3:00 CONVENTION CALLED TO ORDER:
Mrs. A. McD. Wilson, President General, C. S. M. A.
ELECTION OF OFFICERS.
UNFINISHED BUSINESS.
NEW BUSINESS.
ADJOURNMENT.
5:00 to 7:00 TEA AT THE COUNTRY CLUB:
Given by the local Chapters of the United Daughters of the
Confederacy to the Confederated Southern Memorial
Association and the United Daughters of the Confederacy.
9:00 U. C. V. GRAND BALL AT THE GRAYS' ARMORY:
Music by American Legion Band Orchestra.
9:30 BALL IN THE BLUES' ARMORY:
Music by Mississippi State Teachers' College Band. Due to
both armories being very small, this other ball will take
care of the over-flow crowd at the Grays' Armory.
Admission will be by badge or card only.

———

FRIDAY, JUNE 24

10:30 ASSEMBLY FOR GRAND PARADE:
Members of the Confederated Southern Memorial Association
will assemble at the Jefferson Hotel for assignment to
automobiles.
12:00 GRAND PARADE.
9:00 S. C. V. BALL AT THE GRAYS' ARMORY:
Music by local orchestra. Admission by badge or card only.
All members of the United Confederate Veterans and
Confederated Southern Memorial Association are invited
to remain over for this notable event.

———

THIRTY-SEVENTH CONVENTION, SONS OF
CONFEDERATE VETERANS

Opening meeting of the Sons of Confederate Veterans,
Honoring the United Confederate Veterans,
Official Ladies and Members of the
Confederated Southern Memorial
Association

———

TUESDAY, JUNE 21
[*Mosque Auditorium*]
EVENING SESSION

8:00 CONCERT (ending with "Dixie"):
Little Rock High School Band.
8:05 CONVENTION CALLED TO ORDER:
By Hon. Chas. T. Norman, Commander, Stonewall Jackson
Camp No. 981, S. C. V.
8:05 INVOCATION:
Dr. Nathan A. Seagle, New York City, Chaplain-in-Chief,
S. C. V.
8:10 COMMANDER NORMAN TURNS CONVENTION OVER TO
HON. LEE O. MILLER, COMMANDER OF R. E. LEE
CAMP NO. 1, S. C. V.
8:10 COMMANDER MILLER TURNS CONVENTION OVER TO
GEN. R. M. COLVIN, HARRISONBURG, COMMAN-
DER, VIRGINIA DIVISION, S. C. V.
8:15 COMMANDER COLVIN TURNS CONVENTION OVER TO
MAJ. ROBERT S. HUDGINS, RICHMOND, VICE-
COMMANDER-IN-CHIEF FROM ARMY NORTHERN VIR-
GINIA DEPARTMENT, S. C. V., WHO PRESENTS
DR. GEORGE R. TABOR, OKLAHOMA CITY, OKLA.,
COMMANDER-IN-CHIEF, S. C. V.

8:20 COMMANDER-IN-CHIEF TABOR ASSUMES CHAIR AND PRESENTS HON. WALTER L. HOPKINS, RICHMOND, ADJUTANT-IN-CHIEF AND CHIEF OF STAFF, S. C. V., AND THE SPEAKERS OF THE EVENING.
All past commanders-in-chief, all heads of organizations and speakers are expected to be on the stage.

8:25 MALE CHORUS:
Acca Temple Chanters.

8:30 ADDRESS OF WELCOME ON BEHALF OF THE STATE OF VIRGINIA:
His Excellency, Hon. John Garland Pollard, Governor of Virginia.

8:40 ADDRESS OF WELCOME ON BEHALF OF RICHMOND:
Hon. J. Fulmer Bright, Mayor of Richmond.

8:45 ADDRESS OF WELCOME ON BEHALF OF THE UNITED CONFEDERATE VETERANS:
Gen. W. B. Freeman, Honorary Commander-in-Chief, U. C. V., Richmond, Va.

8:50 ADDRESS OF WELCOME ON BEHALF OF THE REUNION COMMITTEE:
Col. Robert T. Barton, Jr., General Chairman.

8:55 RESPONSE TO ADDRESSES OF WELCOME:
Hon. Walter H. Saunders, St. Louis, Mo., Vice Commander-in-Chief, S. C. V., from Army of Trans-Mississippi Department.

9:00 ADDRESS.

9:30 MUSIC, SOUTHERN AIRS:
Capital Choral Club.

9:35 PRESENTATION OF GEN. C. A. DESAUSSURE, MEMPHIS, TENN., COMMANDER-IN-CHIEF, U. C. V.
(Honor guest of the occasion.)

9:40 PRESENTATION OF GEN. HARRY RENE LEE, ADJUTANT-GENERAL AND CHIEF OF STAFF, U. C. V., NASHVILLE, TENN.

9:45 GREETINGS FROM MRS. A. McD. WILSON, OF ATLANTA, GA., PRESIDENT-GENERAL OF THE CONFEDERATED SOUTHERN MEMORIAL ASSOCIATION.

9:50 GREETINGS FROM MRS. W. E. R. BYRNE, OF CHARLESTON, W. VA., PRESIDENT-GENERAL, U. D. C.

9:55 OVERTURE:
Clarksville Boys Band.

10:00 PRESENTATION OF OFFICIAL LADIES:
Hon. John R. Saunders, Attorney-General of Virginia, Richmond, Va.

10:10 RESPONSE FOR OFFICIAL LADIES:
Dr. William R. Dancy, Savannah, Ga., Vice Commander-in-Chief from Army of Tennessee Department, S. C. V.

10:15 "STAR-SPANGLED BANNER:"
Clarksville Boys Band.

10:20 BENEDICTION:
Rev. Ernest Van R. Stires, Richmond, Va.
[Speeches will be limited, as noted above. All Speakers, "Official Ladies" of the United Confederate Veterans and Sons of Confederate Veterans will be expected to be on the stage promptly at 7:45. Admission to stage by card only.]

WEDNESDAY, JUNE 22
MORNING SESSION
[John Marshall Hotel Auditorium]

10:00 MUSIC:
Augusta Police Band.
MEETING CALLED TO ORDER BY DR. GEORGE R. TABOR, COMMANDER-IN-CHIEF, S. C. V.
INVOCATION:
Rev. Nathan A. Seagle, D.D., New York City, Chaplain-in-Chief, S. C. V.
ANNOUNCEMENT OF COMMITTEES TO EXTEND FORMAL GREETING TO THE CONVENTION OF THE UNITED CONFEDERATE VETERANS AND CONFEDERATED SOUTHERN MEMORIAL ASSOCIATION.
GREETINGS FROM:
R. E. LEE CAMP, NO. 1, S. C. V., STONEWALL JACKSON CAMP No. 981, S. C. V. AND WILLIAM I. CLOPTON CAMP No. 530, S. C. V.
Judge Edwin P. Cox, member of R. E. Lee Camp No. 1.

REUNION COMMITTEE:
Edwin H. Courtney, Chairman of Sons Committee.
UNITED CONFEDERATE VETERANS.
UNITED DAUGHTERS OF THE CONFEDERACY.
CONFEDERATED SOUTHERN MEMORIAL ASSOCIATION.
SPANISH WAR VETERANS.
AMERICAN LEGION.
RESPONSE:
Hon. J. S. Utley, Little Rock, Commander, Arkansas Division, S. C. V.
ROLL CALL OF GENERAL OFFICERS AND OF CAMPS OF CONFEDERATION:
Adjutant-in-Chief Walter L. Hopkins.
ANNOUNCEMENT OF CONVENTION COMMITTEES.
REPORTS OF COMMANDERS:
COMMANDER-IN-CHIEF, VICE-COMMANDERS-IN-CHIEF, DIVISION COMMANDERS, BRIGADE COMMANDERS, CAMP COMMANDERS.
REPORTS OF OFFICERS:
INSPECTOR-IN-CHIEF, QUARTERMASTER-IN-CHIEF, COMMISSARY-IN-CHIEF, JUDGE ADVOCATE-IN-CHIEF, SURGEON-IN-CHIEF, HISTORIAN-IN-CHIEF, CHAPLAIN-IN-CHIEF.
REPORTS OF STANDING COMMITTEES:
HISTORICAL, RELIEF, MONUMENT, FINANCE, TEXT-BOOK, MEMORIAL.
REPORTS OF SPECIAL COMMITTEES.
REPORTS OF CONVENTION COMMITTEES.
ANNOUNCEMENTS.
ADJOURNMENT.

AFTERNOON

2:30 LEAVE THE HOTEL JOHN MARSHALL AND GO IN WAITING AUTOMOBILES TO THE DEDICATION OF THE RICHMOND BATTLEFIELD PARKS.

EVENING
[At the Mosque Auditorium]

8:00 RECEPTION IN HONOR OF THE UNITED CONFEDERATE VETERANS, THE CONFEDERATED SOUTHERN MEMORIAL ASSOCIATION AND THE SONS OF CONFEDERATE VETERANS.

[At the Blues' Armory]

9:30 OPENING BALL FOR OFFICIAL GUESTS OF REUNION:
Admittance by badge or card only.

THURSDAY, JUNE 23
MORNING SESSION
[At the John Marshall Hotel]

10:00 MUSIC:
American Legion Band of Nashville, Tenn.
INVOCATION:
Rev. Nathan A. Seagle, D. D., Chaplain-in-Chief, S. C. V.
REPORT OF EXECUTIVE COMMITTEE.
GENERAL BUSINESS.
UNFINISHED BUSINESS.
ADJOURNMENT.

AFTERNOON SESSION

2:30 MUSIC:
Augusta Police Band.
INVOCATION:
Rev. Nathan A. Seagle, D. D., Chaplain-in-Chief, S. C. V.
REPORT OF COMMITTEES.

Awarding of Division Honor Flag.
Unfinished Business.
Election of Officers.
  Commander-in-Chief.
  Vice-Commander-in-Chief, Army Northern Virginia Department.
  Vice-Commander-in-Chief, Army Tennessee Department.
  Vice-Commander-in-Chief, Army Trans-Mississippi Department.
  Historian-in-Chief.
Executive Council:
  Member Army Northern Virginia Department.
  Member Army Tennessee Department.
  Member Army Trans-Mississippi Department.
Adjournment.

EVENING
[*At the Grays' Armory*]

9:00 U. C. V. Grand Ball.
  Admittance to the S. C. V. members by badge or card. Music by American Legion Band Orchestra.

[*At the Blues' Armory*]

9:30 Grand Ball:
  Due to both armories being very small, this ball will take care of the overflow crowd at the Grays' Armory. Admission will be by badge or card only. Music by Mississippi State Teachers College Band.

FRIDAY, JUNE 24
Noon

12:00 Grand Parade:
  The Sons and their "Official Ladies" will leave the Hotel John Marshall and go in waiting automobiles to place designated for the Sons' Section, and will take its place in the parade as it progresses.

EVENING
[*At the Grays' Armory*]

9:00 S. C. V. Grand Ball:
  Admission by ticket and 1932 membership card only, except by those wearing badges (official) of Confederate organizations or in their behalf. Membership card admits self and lady. The Confederate Veterans will be *Special Guests of Honor*.
  All officers and members of the U. C. V. and C. S. M. A. are invited to remain for this notable function.

Special Amusements
[*Camp DeSaussure—Soldiers' Home*]

Corn Cob Pipe of WRVA:
  Pat Binford, Master of Ceremonies.
"That Quartette."
Black Face Artist:
  Bones Driver and George Woodall.
Old Timers:
  Under Direction of Joe Tyler.
Sabbath Glee Club.
Marjorie and George:
  Premier Imitators.
Auto Harp:
  Something Different.
One Man Band:
  A Depression Idea.
Human Saxophone:
  A Jazz Wonder.

Cross Roads Trio:
  Real Harmony.
Ivory Dusters:
  A Musical Treat.
Hack and Sack:
  In Person.
Old Time Fiddlers:
  Under Direction of J. W. Spangler.
"Virginia Reel," "The Minuet" and Specialties:
  East End Junior High School—Under Direction of Mrs. Anne Brame, Mrs. Cecilia L. Myers, Miss Bessie B. Harwood, Mrs. Sidney Swann, at the Piano.
Acca Temple Chanters.
Moving Picture and Lecture—Battle of Gettysburg:
  By Lieut.-Col. T. E. Darby, U. S. A.
"Arion Singers:" Mrs. Emma G. Bell, Soloist; Joseph Whittemore, Soloist; Mrs. W. I. Wilkins, Soloist; Mrs. R. G. Cooper, Soloist:
  Under Direction of Col. E. D. Neff.
Madrigal Quartette:
  Under Direction of Ernest Wilson.
Blue Ridge Mountain Banjo Players.
Historical Pictures and Lectures of Gen. Robert E. Lee and Stonewall Jackson.
  By Mrs. Lottie K. Brown.
Reveille and Retreat Daily.
Daily Band Concerts and Other Amusements.

Other Attractions
[*City of Richmond*]

Daily Band Concerts, Both at Camp DeSaussure and in the City.
Teas at the Country Club and Other Show Places in Richmond.
Placing of the Tablet Commemorating the Inauguration of Jefferson Davis as President of the Confederate States of America.
Dedication of the Richmond Battlefield Parks.
Presentation of the Anchor of the *Virginia-Merrimac* to the Confederate Memorial Literary Society.
Dedication of the New Home for Needy Confederate Women.
Sunset Gun From Capitol Hill, Daily.
Sightseeing Tours of the Battlefields.
Grand Balls.
Receptions.
Presentation of Portrait of Brig.-Gen. Stand Watie, Only Indian Brigadier-General of the Civil War:
  By the Oklahoma Division of the U. D. C. to the Confederate Museum.
Garden Party:
  Maymont, June 22, 4:00 to 6:00 p.m.
Address:
  Gen. S. Gardner Waller.

INTERESTING PLACES TO VISIT

Valentine Museum (Death Mask of Gen. Stonewall Jackson and Recumbent Statue of Gen. Robert E. Lee).
Confederate Museum.
Battle Abbey.
John Marshall Home.
Virginia Historical Society.
Edgar Allan Poe Shrine.
St. Paul's Church.
St. John's Church.
Monumental Church.
Lee House.
Hollywood Cemetery.
Oakwood Cemetery.
Hebrew Cemetery.
Soldiers' Home Museum (Old Sorrell).

The Confederate Tradition
of Richmond

(*Continued from page 33*)

No period of modern history since the Renaissance—not even the French Revolution or the World War—produced so many extraordinary men in a brief four years. It is Richmond's proud distinction that nearly all these great men, with the single exception of General Forrest, were associated with her in some degree while she was the Confederate capital. The greatest of those personalities was that composite of the 150,000 faces and characters which first and last made the private soldier of the Army of Northern Virginia the unique warrior of all the ages. This is not the place to describe him. It would be too long a task to tell of his resourcefulness, his unfailing cheer, his sense of humor, his outlook on life, his devotions and his antipathies, his ability to live on scant rations, his endurance on the march, his democratic discipline, his contempt for cowardice, his ferocity in attack, his inflexibility in the face of adversity. Suffice it to say that the highest monument in Richmond—higher even than that of General Lee—rightly stands to commemorate him as he appeared in the service of the South. Next to him, of course, stands his great commander, the simple soul and the magnificent mind that came to typify in the eyes of the soldiers the ideal that each man secretly shaped for himself. General Lee's associations with Richmond, though brief, are full and rich. His place in history rises with the years. Although he rarely visited the city, if ever, before the war, and was absent from it for long periods during the course of the struggle, it is not too much to say that whatever is fine and aspiring and unselfish and kindly in the life of Richmond is due to this influence more than to that of any other man who ever lived here. His lieutenants and most of his civil associates were worthy of him. One has only to go to the Valentine Museum and look at the death-mask of Stonewall Jackson to realize that under the austerity of the soldier was the spirit of the ascetic.

President Davis was as true a patriot as either of these, without the glory of great victories to soften the final defeat. Tall, erect, with clean-cut, classic features, cursed with ill-health, half blind and handicapped by a singularly-sensitive nature, he bore without a quiver the immense burden of the civil administration. Although his very regard for constitutionalism was held up against him as a vice, when it would have been acclaimed a virtue in another man, he must always be credited with sustaining a struggle that would have ended far sooner without him. If he favored the incompetent Northrop, he sustained the brilliant Gorgas; if he kept Bragg in command when that mistake meant disaster at Lookout Mountain, he likewise retained his faith in Lee after the West Virginia campaign of 1861, and found that faith vindicated.

It is customary to speak of Mr. Davis' cabinet and bureau chiefs as mediocrities, but among them were administrators who would have won distinction in any war—men like Quartermaster General A. R. Lawton, General I. M. St. John, of the Mining and Nitre Bureau, the matchless Gorgas, who has already been mentioned, and the indefatigable Seddon who was incomparably a better Secretary of War than Stanton could ever have been. A portrait gallery of contrasting countenances but common patriotism might be brought together of men like Dr. Bledsoe, Judge J. A. Campbell, General Preston, of the Bureau of Conscription, and a score almost as interesting.

The naval group gave color to the capital—Mallory, Maury, Porter, Davidson, Mitchell, Forrest, Sidney Smith Lee, brother of the general, Semmes, after the loss of the *Alabama*; not to mention Tatnall and Buchanan and those whose duty kept them on the coast. No similar company of naval experts ever made greater contribution to war in as brief a time or under conditions as adverse.

As for the cavalrymen, where was their like? "Jeb" Stuart was the ideal of thousands of young troopers—theatrical, delighting in display, with an unconquerable fondness for sweeping raids, yet a moralist at heart and invincibility correct in his conduct.

His staff lighted many a Richmond party with their gray uniforms and their yellow facings—Heros von Borcke, the von Steuben of the South, Norman FitzHugh, John Esten Cooke, H. B. McClellan, all of them interesting men. Among the brigade and divisional commanders of the cavalry, was there not Wade Hampton? Did not Fitz Lee and his cousin, "Rooney," and "Grumbler" Jones and Rosser and Butler and Robertson and Wickham ride through Richmond streets with rattling sabres?

These are but a few of the personalities that live in Richmond memory seventy years after Joseph E. Johnston marched down from Manassas, and Evans and Lawton came up from the Southern coast for the first great struggle around Richmond. Every name brings up a picture; every career has its inspiration. One finds it difficult to break off when the mention of one leader suggests compeers as valiant and devoted. Surely none can walk the old streets they trod, or read their letters or gaze on their relics in the Confederate Museum and not feel grateful that in that high tradition the humblest son of Richmond can spiritually keep the company of kings.

Objects of Interest in
the Virginia State
Library

(*Continued from page 30*)

times many pay rolls of a single company. A great mass of these pay rolls had been collected in the War Department building in Richmond, the present post office building, and all these were transferred to Washington.

At the present time if any Confederate Veteran in Virginia wishes a certificate of his war record, insofar as these rolls show it, he simply has to write to the Virginia State Library and ask for it.

Probably the most valuable manuscript in the State Library, that is, the manuscript which if sold at auction would command the highest price, is the last dispatch sent to General Lee by Jackson at Chancellorsville. It is not known how this

(*Continued on page 72*)

Capital of the Confederacy

(Continued from page 25)

day, "Nothing was seen, nothing talked of, nothing thought of but the war. Former distinctions were forgotten, old prejudices were laid aside in the universal interest felt in the events of the future, dimmed by the sad prospects of intensive strife. Afflictions, troubles, misfortunes, make all men brothers."

So Richmond, prosperous Richmond, whose trade was flourishing, whose articles were cheap, whose stores were well stocked, settled down to the grim business of war. Soon, very soon, she was to taste of its bitterness.

On Capitol Hill the Confederate government settled down to work. The financial system of the Confederacy gave grave concern. Customs duties were slim because of the blockade. A burdensome war tax, while cheerfully paid, failed to alleviate the necessity of issuing treasury notes and call certificates. The Department of State was striving in vain for foreign recognition. Commissioners were sent abroad. Later congressional committees were to be called upon to investigate the fall of Roanoke Island, the key to Huger's position at Norfolk, and the War Department was to be subjected to the harsh criticism of the press and the public alike. The press grew especially bitter, and editorial attacks were launched against Lee and others in high command.

Heeding the call for more men, the Conscription Act was passed and later was saddled with the Bill of Exemption, loosely constructed measure making possible the abuse of privilege.

Many there were who failed to enjoy the implicit faith of Richmond people and believe that the city was destined to be the permanent seat of the Confederate government. Even General Lee had his doubts, writing in May, 1861, to Mrs. Lee, stopping at the time with her aunt, Mrs. A. M. Fitzhough, ten miles from Arlington:

"If you prefer Richmond, go with Nannie. Otherwise to the Upper Country, as John indicated. I fear I cannot be with you anywhere. I do not think Richmond will be permanent."

And again in October, 1861, following the brilliant victory at Manassas and the comparatively disastrous campaign in the western part of the State:

"If I thought our enemies would not make a vigorous move against Richmond I would recommend to rent a house there."

As the war got under way and the theatre shifted from Big Bethel to Manassas, from Manassas to the Valley, Richmond became a city of refuge. Hospitals appeared on every hill, almost at every corner. Those who could not be cared for in such institutions were welcomed to private homes of the city. Richmond was having her fill of war. Confederate dead and dying were brought from the battlefields where the cry, "On to Richmond!" rattled in the throats of wounded Federals. Windows of Richmond homes shook with the roar of artillery at Seven Pines. Soldiers covered with the blood of battle and the mud from the swamps of the Chickahominy were observed at every turn.

Relieved from the onrush of 1862, Richmond had little cause for rejoicing. Tragedy had touched every home. The blockade was being felt; food was scarce; Richmond was hungry. She had known the dregs of war if not the bitterness of defeat.

The war entered upon its third, its fourth year. Lee was before Petersburg. The morning of April 2 found the sun breaking through a haze that hung over the seven hills of Richmond. It was Sunday and President Jefferson Davis had entered old St. Paul's Church and seated himself in his pew to enjoy the sermon. A messenger made his way up the aisle, stopped before the President and handed him a message signed by Robert E. Lee: "My lines have broken around Petersburg. I can no longer defend Richmond."

The beginning of the end became apparent as preparations were being made to evacuate the Confederate Capital. Excited crowds thronged the streets in search of some means of conveyance. Fire broke out in the tobacco district, swept the length of Main Street, laying waste every building of importance. It was the end. The Capital had fallen. The trail led to Appomattox.

1865-"*The record of the past is the best guarantee for the future*"-**1932**

Rᴵᴄʜᴍᴏɴᴅ'ꜱ *guarantee* for future prosperity is shown by these photographs of the Post Office Building and 10th and Main Streets in 1865 and today.

At the corner shown in the two pictures you will find the *American Bank and Trust Company's Main Bank*. Established in 1899, this strong financial institution has today a capital of $3,500,000 and nine branch banks at selected locations to meet the modern demand for convenience.

The American offers you Capital Strength, Convenience, Courteous Service

★

AMERICAN BANK & TRUST CO.

Richmond « « » » Virginia

Member Clearing House Association of Richmond—Federal Reserve System

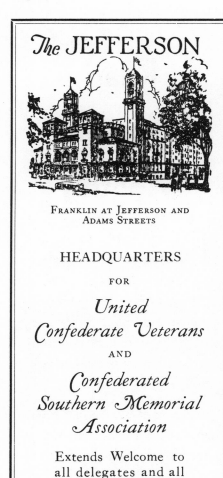
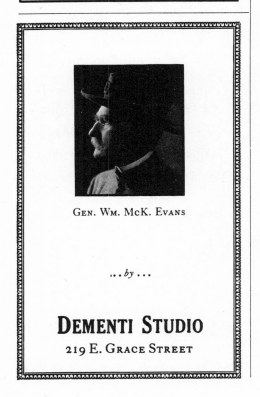
A Sample of Lee's Strategy

(Continued from page 19)

cautious to risk unnecessary frontal attacks upon fortifications. If, therefore, Lee was to gain the time he needed for putting fear into the souls of Banks and Lincoln, and for thus inducing the latter to hold back McDowell, it was all-important that Magruder's lines at Yorktown should not be evacuated too soon, but should remain as an obstacle to McClellan's advance. The latter's progress would have been much swifter if he could have simultaneously used both the York and the James for the transport of troops and supplies up the Peninsula. But the war-vessel, *Virginia* (as the *Merrimac* was called after the Federals had sunk and the Confederates had raised and clad her with iron), stood in McClellan's way, guarding the James against his fleet. Now, since the *Virginia* needed Norfolk as her base, and since the safety of Norfolk depended upon Magruder's fortifications, it was important for these to be held long enough to block McClellan while Lee maneuvered against McDowell, Banks and Frémont, and strengthened the forts on the rivers as well as the fortifications around Richmond.

In order to settle the question whether Yorktown was to be evacuated by Magruder, as Johnston wished, or whether Johnston was himself to be sent there with most of his army, President Davis called a conference of his generals, and, after listening to the discussion, decided in favor of Lee, and sent Johnston to Yorktown.

Just after the conference Lee wrote, on April 21, to Jackson, telling him that the small Confederate force at Fredericksburg was in danger, and saying: "If you can use General Ewell's division in an attack on Banks and to drive him back, it will prove a great relief to the pressure on Fredericksburg." "Here,

then," says Sir Frederick Maurice, "is the genesis of Stonewall Jackson's famous Valley Campaign, and here the first move in Lee's consummate plan for the defense of Richmond." In subsequent letters Lee outlines the further steps which Jackson was to take; always leaving the details to Jackson, while making it plain that his aim should always be to scare Lincoln into keeping McDowell away from Richmond until Lee was ready to summon Jackson himself to join the army there and help to crush McClellan.

It is of course impossible to give an account, in this short article, of the masterly way in which Jackson executed the orders of Lee. But let us consider the effects. On May 3 Johnston, seeing that McClellan was ready to assault his position at Yorktown, fell back toward Richmond, followed by McClellan, who had high hopes of taking the city and ending the war. "On May 21," says Maurice, "Davis was trembling for the safety of Richmond; on the 24th, Jackson's march down the Valley had caused Lincoln to suspend McDowell's movement upon Richmond, and to employ the greater part of his force to take part in a combined movement to capture Jackson and Ewell. Thus the immediate purpose of Lee's maneuver was achieved. On the 25th, Jackson had defeated Banks at Winchester, and occupied the town, and that evening the authorities in

(Continued on page 48)

Lee on Traveller

SERVING THE SOUTH IN THE 60's
SERVING THE NATION TODAY

Left: Thirty-ton wood burning locomotive used by this line during the War Between the States
Below: Present day R. F. & P. locomotive weighing 290 tons

A Pioneer

Five years after the construction of the first successful steam locomotive the Richmond, Fredericksburg and Potomac Railroad Company was chartered, February 25, 1834, and two years later, February 13, 1836, began operating.

Serving the South

In hauling supplies, ammunition and hundreds and thousands of troops and wounded, this railroad rendered invaluable service to the Confederacy during the War Between the States. It bisected and ran in close proximity to some of the greatest battlefields of the War. It was the main line of supply from the Capital of the Confederacy to the battlefields of Northern Virginia. Within 100 yards of its tracks General Stonewall Jackson died, and the house in which he uttered his last words, "Let us pass over the river and rest under the shade of the trees," is now owned by the railroad and preserved as a Confederate shrine.

Ticket issued by the R. F. & P. to be used in returning Confederate soldiers to the lines. Every old soldier knew Sergeant Crowe

Numerous times during the war the road fell in the hands of Federal troops. As each army would be forced to relinquish the line to the other it would do as much damage as possible and at the close of the conflict great stretches of track were torn up, bridges were ashes and in the treasury of the company there were over $700,000 in worthless Confederate Securities but with the indominable spirit of the South the R. F. & P. set about restoring its shattered service and extending its line. Steadily it has grown.

Serving the Nation

And today the R. F. & P. has developed into one of the country's greatest arteries of commerce, the connecting link between the Pennsylvania and Baltimore and Ohio systems and the Atlantic Coast Line and the Seaboard Air Line and connecting the Capital of the Old Dominion with the Capital of the Nation.

See the Points of Historic Interest Along This Line

The Stonewall Jackson Shrine, Guinea Station. The house in which Jackson died, owned by the railroad and preserved as a Confederate Shrine.

Fredericksburg, heart of the famous battlefields of Mayre Heights, Salem Church, Chancellorsville, Spotsylvania and the Wilderness. . . Home of Mary, the Mother of Washington. . . Kenmore, the home of Washington's only sister. . . The homes of John Paul Jones and Matthew Fontaine Maury. . . Rising Sun Tavern. . . Masonic Lodge where Washington was initiated. . . The James Monroe Law Office.

Old Pohick Church, where Washington was a vestryman.

Mount Vernon, the home and the tomb of Washington.

Arlington, the home of Robert E. Lee. . . The National Cemetery which contains the Confederate Soldier's Monument and the Tomb of the Unknown Soldier.

Alexandria, charming old homes. . . Christ Church. . . Site of the George Washington Masonic National Memorial.

Washington, the Nation's Capital.

Avail yourself of the low, round trip rates to Fredericksburg and Washington for the Reunion period and see these never-to-be-forgotten places.

THROUGH such facilities as parlor coaches with luxurious individual seats, pre-cooled sleeping cars during the summer months, and fast schedules, the R. F. & P. offers the most modern comforts to the traveler.

Richmond, Fredericksburg and Potomac Railroad Company

Lee's Strategy

(*Continued from page 46*)

Washington were anticipating an attack upon the Federal capital. Stanton telegraphed to the governors of the Federal States: 'Send forward all the troops you can, immediately. Banks completely routed. Intelligence from various quarters leaves no doubt that the enemy, in great force, are advancing on Washington. You will please organize and forward immediately all volunteer and militia force in your State.' It would be hard to find in the history of war so swift, so dramatic a change of fortune."

Obeying further instructions from Lee, Jackson now drove Banks across the Potomac and swiftly moved back up the Valley, baffling the attempts of Frémont from the west and of Shields from the east to entrap him, and was now in position to obey further orders when the time should come.

Then, on May 31, Johnston attempted, at Seven Pines, to crush McClellan's left wing when separated from his right by the swollen Chickahominy. He gained ground at first, but the well planned battle was not fully successful, and Johnston was severely wounded. Then, on June 1, Lee was put in his place, and from now on controlled both the tactics and the strategy of the army.

Lee let them discover that he was sending troops to Jackson and imagine that the latter might again march toward Washington. McDowell would thus be still kept away from Richmond.

But, as McClellan's army had been much strengthened from other sources, Lee ordered Jackson, on June 17, to join him before McClellan could receive further reinforcements. With such skill did Jackson conceal his departure from the Valley that not till he had joined Lee and the orders for battle had been issued did Secretary Stanton discover the true state of the case. Thus, when Jackson was actually bringing 18,500 men to Lee's aid, Frémont, Banks and McDowell were keeping 70,000 men away from the scene to guard against an imaginary march upon Washington.

There is no space to describe the battle which closed this amazing campaign. Both Lee and Jackson made mistakes in its conduct, and Lee's hope of overwhelming McClellan was not fulfilled. But he did drive him from the Peninsula and defer the capture of Richmond for three years.

When the Tide Flowed

(*Continued from page 21*)

strongly supported by guns, that you were called upon to attack. You fought with bravery and honor, but the task was too great. That night Fitz John Porter withdrew the force which constituted this advanced position, concentrated his main reserve strength, and under Barnard's direction took a position at Gaines' Mill. There you attacked, in much greater numbers than on the day before, a foe that was ready to challenge your advance. On a front two miles long was fought a battle of terrible intensity and magnificent bravery. Lee took a desperate chance in utilizing all his strength north of the Chickahominy to force a favorable decision before nightfall. Finally, a fourth attack near the Watt House succeeded in penetrating the Federal line, and the field of battle was won.

Little thought is given to the small things which sometimes decide a battle. Fitz John Porter had built defensive works to the extent of tools available. These works, on the left, held against three attacks. Had the fourth and last failed, no other could have been made that night. Porter had asked Barnard in the morning to send him more axes from the south side of the Chickahominy. He expected them. They did not come. Without them his log breastworks could not be made stronger.

The battle of Gaines' Mill was one of the most concentrated and deadly of the Civil War. Fitz John Porter's men were packed in a line one and three-quarter miles long. There was a density in the left sector of the position of 25,000 infantry on one mile front. Lee had 50,000 troops opposed to Porter. Seldom did any battle of the World War provide such density.

Gaines' Mill was a day of sorrow to McClellan.   Three telegrams were

sent to Washington in the afternoon and evening, the last at 8:00 o'clock. In the final message McClellan said he would not give up his position north of the Chickahominy "if it is possible to avoid it." Immediately after it was dispatched he learned that the line at Gaines' Mill had been broken. His corps commanders were hurriedly assembled, and before midnight orders were given to the troops north of the Chickahominy to begin crossing to the south side at once. It was not until this moment that the decision was made for the retrogressive flank march of the Army of the Potomac to the James River.

At Savage Station, where the headquarters of his army were moved from the Trent house, McClellan at midnight sent the message to Stanton in which he said: "If I save my army now, I tell you plainly that I owe no thanks to you or to any other persons in Washington. You have done your best to sacrifice this army." This dispatch bares a soul tortured with the unknown fear of a first gigantic failure. Brought to this high command from successes in Western Virginia which won praise from the President, the Cabinet, the general-in-chief, and the people, this proud idol of the army had led his men up to the very gates of victory, only to be rebuffed, battered, and beaten back from the goal so enticingly near.

"Save your army at all events," was the order that came to him from the President the next day, accompanied by the comment, "If you have had a drawn battle or a repulse it is the price we pay for the enemy not being in Washington." The movement to the James River demonstrated McClellan's ability as a tactician and strategist, and became the foundation stone of Lee's great military reputation.

On the day after Gaines' Mill the Federal divisions were shifted to cover the withdrawal of the troops and transportation to a new base. The Confederate forces were engaged in seeking information as to the movements and intentions of McClellan's command. The 29th of June

brought on the action at Savage Station between the corps of Magruder, supported by Huger, which had been left on the right bank of the Chickahominy, and part of McClellan's army in that locality.

On the 30th occurred that terrible action at Glendale or Frayser's Farm. The battle line extended from White Oak Swamp, through Glendale to Malvern Hill, a deployment seven miles long. Jackson's command, which now included the corps of D. H. Hill, could not get into the main part of the fight. Holmes had a minor engagement at Malvern Hill. At Frayser's Farm A. P. Hill's command, which had been heavily engaged at Beaver Dam Creek and Gaines' Mill, and Longstreet's troops, also engaged at Gaines' Mill, assailed a strong Federal line of infantry supported by powerful artillery. The fighting quality of these troops was so superior that they took batteries in hand to hand combat, without the aid of a single supporting gun.

When this terrific onslaught terminated with the night, McClellan succeeded in withdrawing his train of 2,500 wagons to safety in the rear of Malvern Hill. Here he took position with his entire army, covering the rim and entrance of a plateau of immense extent. Lee hurled the greater part of his army against the level entrance to the plateau, and the final battle of the Seven Days' campaign brought additional undying glory to both armies. That night the Northern army withdrew to the site which had been selected on the James River for its new base.

The strength of the Army of the Potomac on June 20, 1862, not including the men absent, was 117,226 men and 316 pieces of artillery. The number of troops under the command of General Lee was a little less than 90,000. No consolidated report has ever been compiled. The reported Federal losses in the Seven Days' Battles in killed, wounded, captured, and missing were 15,849. The forces commanded by Lee had 20,076 reported casualties.

Thus it was that the tide of battle was swept back from Richmond. At no other period of the war, until the end, was the capital of the Confederacy so endangered.

You, Veterans of this and other glorious battlefields of the gigantic struggle, the South salutes. Yes, the North, too, bows in reverence.

And I, a soldier of later wars, will always feel that the War for Independence and the War Between the States are the greatest in the history of our country.

Petersburg's Three Hundred Days

(*Continued from page 29*)

to cut the Weldon Railroad, and thus deprive Beauregard of reinforcements from the South. In this effort, Kautz was not successful and he did not attack Petersburg, but General Pickett, then in command here, garrisoned the Dimmock line with his 600 regulars and 600 militia to meet an attack.

THE 9TH OF JUNE, 1864: The first real attack upon the city was made on June 9, 1864, by 4,500 of Butler's troops under General Gillmore and General Kautz. Gillmore's 300 infantry and Kautz's 1,500 cavalry crossed the pontoon bridge across the Appomattox at Broadway on the morning of June 9th, and advanced against the city. Gillmore's infantry came along the City Point Road. The skirmishers were driven in, the picket lines were taken, and for the first time Battery 5 faced attack. General Wise was now in charge of the defense of the city and he had only 1,200 men to man the six miles of entrenchments from the Appomattox to the Jerusalem Plank Road. By some quirk of fate, Gillmore did not attack.

THE RIVES SALIENT: Not so, however, with Kautz's cavalry. Crossing early on this same 9th of June at Broadway, Kautz's 1,500 men made a wide detour and advanced against the city from the south along the Jerusalem Plank Road. Two miles from town, the Dimmock line guarded this road at Battery 27, the Rives Salient, to which the militia and reserves were summoned post haste. Of the six militia companies of Capt. F. H. Archer's battalion, only 125 men arrived in time to face the sudden attack. Wise's 1,200 regulars were holding the eastern line of defense, but it was a mile from Archer's militia to Wise's troops on the east and on

AWAITING HIS MEN

ON RICHMOND'S beautiful Monument Avenue stands this symbol, a commanding equestrian statue of Gen. Robert E. Lee, awaiting the forty-second reunion of his men.

From the length and breadth of Dixieland come these heroes to visit again the city so rich in Confederate history . . . to visit again the Capital of the Confederacy . . . to enjoy again Richmond's world-famous hospitality.

Lee's men and their families will find a warm welcome in our hearts and in our homes, now as always. Welcome—and come again soon!

VIRGINIA ELECTRIC AND POWER COMPANY

the west of Archer the empty lines stretched four miles back to the river. The old men and boys knew that the fate of the city depended on them. They were bankers and ministers, druggists and editors, manufacturers and merchants, exempt through age, and also the youngsters of the town. Several of them were teachers, one the writer's father, who had three sons in active service.

The "local force" repulsed two attacks of Kautz's cavalry, but Kautz then dismounted his men and advanced on front and flank, his lines overlapping the militia lines on right and left flank. For two hours the stubborn fight went on, until Archer's men, facing the original front of attack, were shot from the rear and a retreat was ordered. But these two hours of fighting enabled Graham's battery and Dearing's cavalry to reach the city in time to check the raid in the very suburbs. Of the 125 defenders, sixty-seven were killed or wounded or captured, more than half, and it is in memory of these sons that Petersburg holds its Memorial Day on the 9th of June.

BATTERY 5: About a week after Kautz's Raid, on June 15th, a second attempt was made to seize the city by a surprise attack. By this time Wise had 2,200 men to man his lines. Against them Butler sent from Bermuda Hundred his 18th Corps under General "Baldy" Smith, just back from Cold Harbor, where it had reinforced Grant. Smith's column of 16,000 landed at Bermuda Hundred from transports on the night of the 14th, advanced early on the 15th over the pontoon bridge at Broadway, and moved in three columns along the Jordan Point and City Point roads. Kautz's cavalry, now 2,400 strong, came with them. The Confederate skirmishers and outposts of cavalry and artillery delayed the advance, but by two o'clock the attack began on Battery 5 and the redans to right and left. Twice the strong rifle pits in front of Battery 5 were taken and retaken and at the third assault the garrison leaped the parapet and again drove back the Federals.

It was not until seven o'clock of the hot, dusty June day that Smith finally launched his successful attack through a deep ravine, captured Battery 6

and took Battery 5 through the open rear. By nine o'clock the Union troops had taken Batteries 3 to 11, inclusive, a mile and a half of entrenchments with sixteen guns and several hundred prisoners. Through this wide gap in the Dimmock line the Federals began to advance against Wise's new line on the next ridge, when Hagood's South Carolina brigade and Hoke's North Carolina division "came in at the double-quick and stopped the break." Hancock's Federal Corps of the Army of the Potomac arrived at this time, and this overwhelming force of nearly forty thousand could have taken the city by a prompt advance, but Smith decided to defer the attack until the next day. So dire was the need of defenders that Beauregard withdrew his forces from "bottling up" Butler in the Bermuda Hundred lines and threw them into the Petersburg lines that night in time to meet the combined assaults of Smith and Hancock and Warren the next day. The militia had done well, Wise had done well, now it was "up to" Beauregard. Archer's men saved Petersburg on June 9th, Wise on the 15th, Beauregard on the 16th and 17th, Lee on the 18th.

This four-day Battle of Petersburg lasted from the 15th to the 18th of June and it cost the Union forces 10,000 men. It was not only a stern and bitter series of battles, but also a dramatic series of foot-races, for the reason that Lee was wary of sending his troops from the Richmond lines to Petersburg and finally had to use desperate haste to remedy the delay. "One of Grant's four great achievements," says a recent writer, "was that for three days he gave the slip to Robert E. Lee."

The gallant and desperate nature of the fighting on both sides on June 18 is attested by the inscription on the granite monument in front of Colquitt's Salient, in memory of the First Maine Heavy Artillery. This is between Battery 5 and Fort Stedman. In their assault on Colquitt's Salient, "604 brave members fell charging here on June 18, 1864."

FORT STEDMAN AND GRACIE'S SALIENT: As the crow flies, it is only two miles from Battery 5 via the

Welcome, Veterans!

TO THE SURVIVING COMRADES of the Confederacy's gray-clad armies who will convene in Richmond this month for their forty-second annual reunion, The Life Insurance Company of Virginia gives hospitable welcome and a proud salute.

May renewal of old friendships, reminiscence of stirring days, and the affection of a city whose streets once resounded to their martial footsteps make their sojourn memorably pleasant.

1871   The LIFE INSURANCE COMPANY of VIRGINIA   1932

BRADFORD H. WALKER, *President*

Maine Monument to Fort Stedman, but as time flies, it is nine months and ten days. In the interval, this strong Union work, Fort Stedman, was built about on the spot wh ere the battle were fought for the Hare House in the early days of the siege. On one side the Federal Fort Haskell looms through the trees, on the other side stretches the strong line of Federal batteries to the river, and behind it are other works protecting Grant's military railroad to City Point.

Facing Fort Stedman are two Confederate works guarding both sides of the ridge. On one slope is Colquitt's Salient and on the other Gracie's Salient, with its dam of Poo Creek protecting the Haskell front. This is a strong point of the lines. Every ridge has its redoubt and every slope climbs to a battery. It is the grim visage of war.

One week before the end of the siege, on March 25, 1865, Lee sent Gordon with "a well-selected body of Confederates" against Fort Stedman in a desperate effort to break Grant's lines east of the city, to cut Grant's City Point railroad, and thus to relieve the pressure on the west. Lee's purpose was also to force Grant to withdraw his left and leave the Cox Road open for retreat. It was "the last grand offensive movement of the Army of Northern Virginia."

From Fort Stedman, it is only two miles past Fort Haskell and Fort Morton to the Baxter Road and the Crater. This is the site of the "Petersburg Mine" and of the notable fight of July 30, 1864. As the name indicates, the Crater is the "Hole-in-the-Ground" left by the explosion of 8,000 pounds of powder under an advanced Confederate work, Elliott's Salient. The mine was prepared by Burnside's Pennsylvania miners, and the explosion was planned to open a way through the breach in the Confederate lines to Cemetery Ridge and to the city. Sixty-five thousand Union troops were massed for the attack. The mine was exploded at 4:30 a.m. on July 30, 1864, killing the 250 men in Elliott's Salient, and the Federal troops advanced into and through the Crater, and seized the lines for some distance on each side. Their advance was checked, however, by the fire of the Confed-

erate batteries to right and left of the Crater and other Federal troops coming to the support of the first attacking column fell into confusion and also took refuge in the pit of the Crater.

There were no troops between the Crater and Petersburg. The way to the city was open, save for the enfilading batteries. Four brigades of Mahone's Division, in four gallant charges from 9:00 to 1:00 o'clock, recaptured the Crater and the lines to the north and south of it. The Federal loss was over five thousand, the Confederate loss about one thousand.

"Hell" and "Damnation:" There are many Confederate Tunnels in front of the Rives Salient, where the first attack was made on the city on the 9th of June of 1864. This Salient was Battery 27, next to it on the west was Battery 28, and next was Battery 29, later Fort Mahone. Facing these on the Federal line was Fort Sedgwick. So fierce was the fighting along this much-contested stretch of the Jerusalem Plank Road that Fort Sedgwick was nicknamed "Fort Hell," Fort Mahone became "Fort Damnation," even little Battery 28 became "And," so that here "the road to Jerusalem ran between 'Hell' 'And' 'Damnation.'"

Fort Gregg: On this same 2d of April, the day after Five Forks, where Lee's lines had been broken in the west, the advance of the Federals from Fort Fisher was halted by the Confederate Fort Gregg. This was a small fort with steep embankment and ditch, but closed in the rear only with a fence. Two hundred and fifty men held this fort against Gibbon's Union troops attempting to break through to the city. When it was at last taken, only thirty defenders were left and 714 of the enemy had fallen. This heroic defense was one of the most desperate of the War. Even after Fort Gregg was captured, as Gibbon says, "the (Federal) troops were ordered to retire from the work to prevent further sacrifice," and thus the inner line of the Petersburg defense remained unbroken to the evacuation.

It was from the Federal Fort Fisher, a few miles south of Fort

(Continued on page 68)

Dementi Photo

The Confederate Memorial Institute

Tourist Guide to Richmond

(*Continued from page 37*)

the lower manufacturing district. Van Lew Home Site. Returning by way of Grace Street, the site of the Chief Federal Secret Service Agent's home will be found at Twenty-Fourth Street. Miss Elizabeth Van Lew furnished the Northern Army with valuable information throughout the war.

St. John's Church. Just around the corner, occupying an entire block, at Twenty-Fourth and Broad Streets, is the famous St. John's Church, where Patrick Henry, on March 20, 1775, awakened the world with his plea, "Give me liberty or give me death." A bronze tablet marks the pew from which he spoke, in the presence of George Washington, Thomas Jefferson, John Marshall and others, who played leading roles in America's history. The church was opened first

in 1741, and in its burying ground will be found many ancient tombstones, the oldest being that of Rev. Robert E. Rose, 1751. Elizabeth Arnold Poe, mother of Edgar Allan Poe, is buried here.

MASON'S HALL. On Franklin Street, near Nineteenth, is the oldest Masonic Hall in the United States. Governor Edmund Randolph assisted in laying the foundation in 1785, and Lafayette was given a reception there in 1824. The hall was used as a military hospital in 1812. It has been occupied continuously since 1787 by Richmond Randolph Lodge, No. 19. When the Northern troops entered the city, April 3, 1865, this was one of the first buildings around which guards were stationed.

LIBBY PRISON SITE. Two blocks to the south and one to the east, at Twentieth and Cary Streets, is the site of Libby Prison, probably the best known of Confederate prisons. It was national in reputation. Some thirty years ago a Chicago capitalist purchased the building with the intention of tearing it down and re-

Demetri Photo

erecting it in his home town. Several train loads of material were wrecked and lost while in transit and all that Chicago has of the relic is its "atmosphere," which it is to be hoped is purer than in the days when it housed those in "durance vile." Libby was used exclusively for officers, and it is said that more men passed through it than any other military prison.

EDGAR ALLAN POE SHRINE. The old stone house at 1916 East Main Street, built in 1737 by Jacob Ege, a German silversmith, was Lafayette's headquarters in Richmond, and both Presidents Washington and Monroe were entertained there. It has been beautified and improved recently and now houses many things associated with the life and memory of the great Southern poet and writer. To appreciate fully the historic shrines of Richmond the visitor is urged to allot time for a careful tour.

Lee Statue, Monument and Allen Avenues

Demetri Photo

Jackson Statue, Monument Avenue and the Boulevard

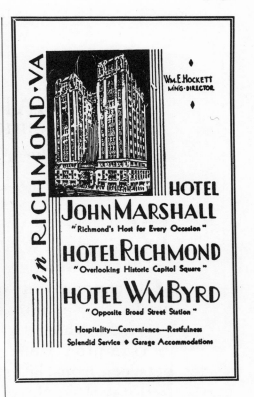

Federal Raids on the Confederate Capital

(Continued from page 31)

Three belts of defense encircled the city and with an adequate force to man the works, they seemed impregnable.

The spring of 1863 found Lee facing Hooker across the Rappahannock. The Federal commander sought a diversion by dispatching Stoneman, his cavalry chief, on a raid of Lee's communications. The cavalry corps, dispatched from the main operations of the Army of the Potomac, had orders to skirt Lee's left and inflict all possible injury.

On May 3, 1863, Stoneman divided his force into six parts and penetrated well into Confederate territory. Reaching Ashland, the main body was checked by Gen. W. H. F. Lee.

While Lee's communications were cut only briefly, the action had undoubtedly the effect of alarming the country through which the columns moved and caused consternation in the capital. Much property was destroyed, but this was offset by the loss to Hooker of his "eyes" when they were most needed at Chancellorsville, possibly enabling Jackson to execute his secret concentration opposite the Federal right.

Of an entirely different nature was the Kilpatrick-Dahlgren thrust at Richmond, the objective of which was to release the thousands of prisoners on Belle Isle and in Libby Prison, the destruction of military and personal property and the probable capture or killing of the Confederate civil leaders.

Kilpatrick was the commander of the raiding force of more than 4,000 men, but the spectacular and daring part of the expedition was in the hands of Col. Ulric Dahlgren, a twenty-two-year-old cavalryman who already had sacrificed a leg for his country and was destined to pay for his part in the raid with his life.

General Meade assisted the venture by a demonstration against Lee's left and by sending Custer on a minor raid into Albemarle. On the night of February 28, the Federal force started. At Spotsylvania Court House Dahlgren and his picked band of 500 men detached themselves from the

main body for the purpose of crossing the James River and attacking Richmond suddenly from the south, while the others struck simultaneously from the north.

Dahlgren destroyed everything in his path as he dashed across the country. A negro guide's faithfulness to his master, however, was the undoing of the intrepid young leader, for instead of taking him to a crossing point, he guided the Federals into Goochland, miles from the objective. Learning of what he considered treachery, Dahlgren ordered the negro hanged and his own bridle was said to have been used for this grim purpose.

Dahlgren then moved swiftly towards Richmond on the north bank. Again Providence stepped in to interfere with the plans. A message from Dahlgren to Fitzpatrick arranging for the simultaneous attack on the city was intercepted and the details of the Federal plans became known.

Meanwhile Fitzpatrick on February 29 struck Beaver Dam Station and burned it, together with a large amount of Confederate supplies. He was prevented, however, from wrecking the railroad bridge across the South Anna. The following day he was before the fortifications of Richmond. The swoop had been so sudden that the Federal troopers passed within the outer line of redoubts unopposed, but stopped in sight of the second line.

The Federal approach had been along the Meadow Bridge Road and Brook Turnpike. As Kilpatrick hesitated within three miles of the city, General Wilcox organized all men on furlough and civilians able to bear arms and rushed them to the fortifications. Gen. Wade Hampton suddenly appeared with his troops and Kilpatrick fell back rapidly, losing many, killed and wounded, and 350 prisoners.

The Dahlgren party continued to near Richmond from the west. He struck the outer line at dark on March 2. Not hearing from his superior, he determined to attack, but the volunteer force surprised him with the vigor of its defense at a point along the Cary Street Road, now marked suitably. Dahlgren's force retreated, making an attempt to sweep around the Confederates to the Peninsula. The force became divided, Dahlgren leading one body into King and Queen County, where, on March 3, he was ambushed by troops under Lieut. James Pollard near Walkerton. On the first fire, Dahlgren was killed instantly. Practically his whole column was taken.

The Kilpatrick-Dahlgren raid was the second unsuccessful one made that spring. General Butler had formed the plan of sweeping down on the Confederate capital by way of New Kent Court House. As a diversion the Army of the Potomac, was to make a demonstration across the Rapidan.

The raiding column under Wister left New Kent on February 5 and reached the Chickahominy at Bottom's Bridge. He found the crossing blockaded and after a reconnoissance in force he fell back and Butler's scheme was abandoned. The Richmond home guard, however, had been rushed to the defense lines to repel the expected attack.

Meanwhile Kilpatrick crossed the Rapidan. He found the Confederates able to take care of themselves and retreated with the loss of 250 men. It was said that this reverse made him the more eager to conduct the later expedition.

The most important raid aimed at Richmond and one that was highly disastrous to the Confederate cause, as it was a prelude to the death of the dashing Stuart, was engineered shortly after by Sheridan. The expedition was a short but destructive one, but without important military results, although it answered its purpose of pulling the menacing Virginia cavalry off the Federal supply trains.

Sheridan, with 10,000 men stretching thirteen miles in column, crossed the North Anna on May 9, 1864. Again Beaver Dam Station was taken and the railroad for ten miles was destroyed, along with rolling stock and Confederate food supplies. Stuart with his numerically smaller force was harassing the invader continually, but on May 11 the Federal cavalry reached Ashland and destroyed another six miles of railroad and military stores.

Sheridan's mission was to menace Richmond and to gain contact with Butler at the Army of the James.

Continuing toward Richmond, Sheridan met Stuart and two brigades at Yellow Tavern the same day. Stuart's 3,000 men were driven back with the loss of the brave leader and Gen. J. B. Gordon, who likewise received a mortal wound. Sheridan pressed on and penetrated the outer works, just as Kilpatrick had done previously. He could see the lights of Richmond and hear the barking of watch dogs, but his single attack was repulsed as the Confederates threw in reinforcements from the forces holding Butler in check at Bermuda Hundred. Sheridan dropped back, fighting another engagement when he met a force disputing his passage of the Chickahominy at Meadow Bridge. Sheridan reached Haxall's Landing where he procured supplies and then returned to the Army of the Potomac by way of White House on the Pamunkey. Grant in a dispatch said Sheridan had passed entirely around Lee's army in his sixteen-day operation.

After Cold Harbor, Grant's activities were transferred south of the James River and for the time being the pressure against Richmond was lessened. While the menace was great, the presence of Lee's main body in front of Grant relieved the anxiety in the city.

The spring of 1865 found abortive attempts against the capital becoming more frequent. Constant calls were made on the volunteer forces, but no real attacks developed. The fighting was restricted almost entirely to the vicinity of Petersburg, with leaders recognizing that the fate of the capital depended upon the outcome there.

Such was the situation on the Sunday morning in April when President Davis received the bitter word from Lee that the time to abandon Richmond had come. The alarmed city awaited the inevitable and the next appearance of the foe was uncontested and he entered a devastated and broken shell of a city.

Richmond Battlefield Parks
(Continued from page 35)

The Conservation and Development Commission is erecting on the battlefield route iron markers giving information of the Seven Days' Battles in 1862 and a number of temporary wooden markers describing the campaign of 1864. When the park shall have been developed, visitors will be able to go over the whole field with ease and see the positions of the various commands and generals. It is probable that novel features will be incorporated in this park that will make more vivid and engrossing the presentation of history.

South of the James River, the park includes Fort Darling at Drewry's Bluff. There, on the height immediately overlooking the river, the Confederates constructed the chief water defense of Richmond. Great guns frowned from the fort, while in the river below ships were sunk to block the channel. A Union squadron tried to sail past Drewry's Bluff on May 15, 1862, but was repulsed. Thereafter Richmond was not seriously threatened from the water.

Fort Darling is a very beautiful spot, a little gem of a park.

On February 23, 1932, in the presence of the Virginia Assembly, the Richmond Battlefield Parks area was formerly turned over to the State. The park is now included in the Division of Parks of the Conservation and Development Commission, which is about to make a complete survey of the area with the purpose of developing it along the latest lines of park development. When the park is completed, Richmond will have the most beautiful military park in America, if not in the world.

Behind this bare statement of facts lies a story of patriotic endeavor and civic accomplishment that should make the citizens of Richmond proud of their city. For the inception of the Battlefield Park came from Richmond citizens, who raised the money acquired the land, and then turned over the project to the State for the benefit of the people of the whole United States.

T. M. Carrington, president of the Richmond Battlefield Parks Corporation, J. Ambler Johnston, Dr. Douglas S. Freeman, and their associates, who included many of the public-minded men and women of Richmond, carried this great accomplishment to fruition, acquiring nearly five hundred acres of land in the vicinity of Richmond closely associated with the scenes of the War Between the States. The man who did the actual work of negotiation, who gave his skill and enthusiasm to the effort, has gone from us—John C. Easley, who met a tragic death several years ago.

Fredericksburg
(*Continued from page 22*)

Shortly after arriving at Warrenton, McClellan was relieved by Burnside. Burnside elected to move on Fredericksburg and base his operations against Richmond on the R. F. & P. Railroad. Answering this move, Lee sent Longstreet's Corps to that town, and shortly after moved Jackson's Corps from the Valley and it took up a position on the south bank of the Rappahannock, eastward as far as Port Royal.

Burnside's plan was to attack Lee's army before it could be put into a

position of defense. It failed because of tardy and bungling execution. When Burnside began the crossing of the Rappahannock on the 11th of December, 1862, Lee's army was strung out between Fredericksburg and Port Royal. The obstacles to be overcome before a crossing of the river on pontoon bridges could be effected delayed the attack till the 13th of December and gave Jackson's Corps time to get into position, so that when the attack was finally made Lee had his army concentrated on the hills southwest of the town. Even as the battle opened on the 13th, Burnside displayed entire lack of the qualities for supreme command, exhibiting bewilderment and vacillation. After considerable hesitation, he launched his splendid brigades against the almost impregnable Confederate positions. It was a fruitless sacrifice of valor, which Burnside's officers dissuaded him from repeating on the following day. On the night of the 15th he withdrew unmolested to the north bank of the Rappahannock.

Mr. Lincoln, still in search of the man with the capacity of supreme command, relieved Burnside and put Hooker in his place, January 26, 1863. The Confederates still occupied the south bank of the Rappahannock. Hooker did fine work in reorganizing his army and restoring its morale, and by the latter part of April was ready to begin his main movement against Lee. He commanded 130,000 men with which to oppose Lee's 60,000. His first move was to send part of his army under Sedgwick to distract Lee's attention, by crossing the Rappahannock below Fredericksburg, while the main Union Army crossed above Fredericksburg. This ruse was successfully executed. He had crossed the Rapidan at Ely's and Germanna Fords before Lee was aware of his designs. During the night of April 30 Hooker concentrated his main army at Chancellorsville, on Lee's left flank.

Lee, having ascertained Hooker's designs, took prompt steps to meet the menace of this situation. Longstreet was ordered to Chancellorsville, and Jackson to Hamilton's Crossing. On May 1, Hooker started three columns on the roads towards Fredericksburg. Halfway between Chan-

cellorsville and Salem Church they came into contact with the Confederate forces moving on Chancellorsville and some indecisive fighting ensued.

At this point Hooker, for some incomprehensible reason, timidly drew in his forces, and with his splendid army, outnumbering his foe more than two to one, assumed the defensive and entrenched himself in the wilderness about Chancellorsville.

Lee now marched up and took a position confronting Hooker on a line extending northeast and southwest about a mile from Chancellorsville. At this point Lee, face to face with a hugely preponderant army, adopted a battle plan of almost unparalleled audacity. He ordered Jackson who has been stationed on his right with 30,000 men to make a wide detour through the wilderness and fall upon Hooker's exposed right flank. After a march of fifteen miles, the dust of his columns being visible to the enemy who mistook it for a retreat, the punctual Jackson, at 6:00 p.m., fell upon the exposed rear and flank of Howard's Corps and stampeded it in panic through the woods. The intervening darkness and the wounding of Jackson saved the Federal army from overwhelming disaster. Lee had laid a wager on the supine ineptitude of Hooker and had won. Stuart took command of Jackson's Corps and attacked Hooker the next morning from the west. By noon he had occupied Chancellorsville. Hooker retired into the wilderness and entrenched himself heavily. He abandoned the offensive without putting several of his Corps into action at all.

While these great events were being transacted, Sedgwick had driven Early out of Fredericksburg and was marching on Chancellorsville. Lee, on learning this, sent a division to oppose him. This division, at Salem Church on May 3, ended Sedgwick's advance. A few days later he and Hooker were reunited on the north bank of the Rappahannock. Lee had shown himself Hooker's master at every phase of the battle. Plainly, Hooker would not do.

In early May Grant began his movement toward Richmond from Culpeper, across a portion of the battlefield of Chancellorsville. His pre-ponderance in artillery made it greatly to his advantage to fight in the open, and his object was to get through the wilderness before Lee could come up with him. Lee was too alert. When Grant began to move, he started the corps of Ewell and Hill to intercept him in the wilderness. By the 5th of May these two corps were three and a half miles from the enemy. Early next morning Ewell's Corps and Griffin's Division of the Union Fifth Corps came into contact on the Orange Court House road, and a fierce but indecisive battle raged across this road most of the day, Ewell's Corps opposing the Union Fifth and Sixth Corps, under Warren and Sedgwick.

While this was transpiring, A. P. Hill, moving on the old Orange Plank Road, encountered Getty's Division of the Sixth Corps, and the fight that followed momentarily menaced Grant's plans, and forced him to hurry up Hancock's Second Corps to prevent Hill from taking possession of the important junction of the Plank

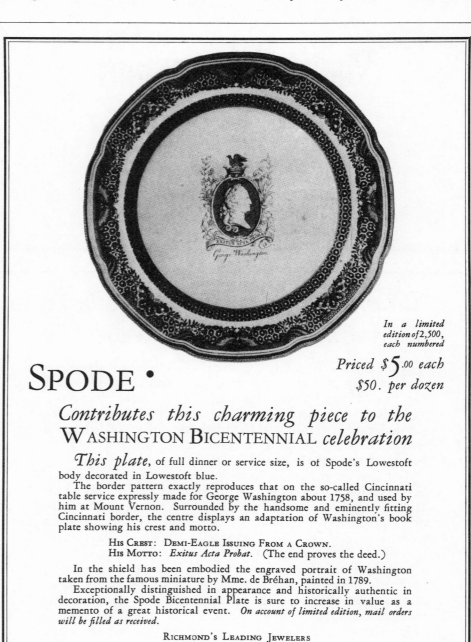

Visit Historic Fredericksburg

BATTLEGROUND OF THE CONFEDERACY

HISTORIC FREDERICKSBURG, within approximately an hour's drive of Richmond, headquarters for the Forty-second Annual Confederate Reunion, extends to the veterans of the 'sixties, to the Sons of Confederate Veterans and to members of the Confederated Southern Memorial Association an invitation to visit her numerous shrines and battlefields.

The five great battles of the War Between the States—Salem Church, Chancellorsville, Spotsylvania C. H., Fredericksburg and the Wilderness—were waged within or immediately adjacent to the city. These sites are now included in the beautiful National Battlefield Memorial Park project.

Colonial as well as Confederate history was written in Fredericksburg. Washington was intimately associated with the city. Here the home and grave of his mother are located and here stands Kenmore, the home of his sister. The office in which James Monroe practiced law stands in a perfect state of preservation, and other historic shrines abound in this historic city.

Visit Fredericksburg Following the Reunion

FREDERICKSBURG CHAMBER OF COMMERCE

Road with the Brock Road. Lee had ordered Hill to take possession of this cross-road, and Hancock's Corps came up just in time to prevent it. Hill was pushed back to Parker's Store. The battle then stabilized here as it had on the Orange Court House Road. Both sides intrenched and consolidated their lines.

Early the next morning Hancock advanced on the Plank Road against Hill and was at the point of driving him from his entrenched position when Longstreet's Corps, having marched all night, arrived from Mechanicsville, and was immediately thrown into action, Lee assuming personal command.

Hancock's forces had become disorganized in the thickets, and Longstreet struck them with violence, flank and rear, and one of the war's worst scenes of carnage ensued. Thousands were killed, the woods took fire, and many of the wounded were burned to death.

At the crisis of the battle Longstreet was wounded and, as at Chancellorsville, the disabling of the commander marred the fruition of Confederate victory. In the resulting confusion Lee stopped the attack. This gave Hancock time to reorganize so that on the following morning he was able to stop an attack in its tracks.

Lee now hurried to his left flank and conferred with Ewell and Gordon, with the result that Gordon moved off through the woods toward the northeast and made a surprise attack on the Sixth Corps, throwing it into a near panic and forcing it to retreat to high ground near the old Wilderness Tavern, where it entrenched. The following day both armies rested from their exertions, and that night Grant resumed his inexorable march on Richmond, selecting Spotsylvania Court House as his next objective.

At once Lee began to move to intercept him. Grant marched on the Brock Road. Two brigades of Lee's cavalry reached Spotsylvania Court House ahead of the columns of either army. One of these took a position across the Brock Road and delayed Warren's Fifth Corps which was leading Grant's advance. This permitted Lee's leading units, which had marched over a trail cut through the Wilderness, some distance from the

Brock Road, to reach Spotsylvania Court House ahead of Warren.

The Confederate forces deployed across the Brock Road in two entrenched battle lines. Warren's Fifth Corps deployed to the right of the Brock Road and the Sedgwick's Sixth Corps to the left. In the fighting here, General Sedgwick was killed by a Confederate sharpshooter.

Grant, bringing up Hancock's Second Corps, now attempted to turn Lee's left flank. In doing so, Hancock crossed the Po River and became involved in the marshes along its bank, which caused Grant to order his withdrawal to the north of the Po.

On the 10th of May the Sixth Corps, now under command of Upton, began a furious assault against the Confederate lines at a point now famous in history as "The Bloody Angle." The angle was caused by the location of Ewell's line on a ridge which stuck out at an angle in a southeasterly direction. Upton captured part of the Confederate trenches at this point but was forced to withdraw in the night.

Grant now moved his Second Corps from his right flank to his left, and on May 12, in a violent storm of rain, launched a furious mass attack against the very point of the Confederate angle. Hancock and Upton broke through the Confederates at this point and occupied their lines. For over thirty hours the army of Lee pressed an unavailing counter attack, until the Confederate General, satisfied of the futility of further assault, withdrew his troops from the angle and constructed a line along its base.

After some further fighting around Spotsylvania Court House of a desultory and inconclusive character, Grant again moved around Lee's right flank to the south and east, and the battle passed out of Spotsylvania County, on toward the final curtain of the great drama.

Within this war-torn area, the Civil War casualties, killed, wounded and missing, were: Union, 92,479; Confederate, 37,257, making a total of 129,736.

The Sixty-Ninth Congress passed an act entitled: "An act to establish a national Military Park at and near Fredericksburg, Virginia, and to mark and preserve historical points, con-

nected with the battles of Fredericksburg, Spotsylvania Court House, Wilderness and Chancellorsville, including Salem Church, Virginia."

On October 19, 1928, President Coolidge dedicated the park with a speech at Mansfield Hall Country Club at Fredericksburg.

The work of carrying out the provisions of the act establishing the park is under the direction of the Fredericksburg and Spotsylvania Battlefield Memorial Commission, comprised of Maj.-Gen. John L. Clem, U. S. A., chairman; Hon. R. Walton Moore, member, and Maj. Arthur E. Wilbourn, U. S. A., member and secretary.

Major Wilbourn has his offices in Fredericksburg and the execution of the plan is under his direction. It is to him that the writer is indebted for the material contained in this article.

The work is one requiring much minute and detailed study. When it is done the history of these great battles will be made legible for posterity, and not be lost in the limbo of legend and sentimental saga.

The Granary of the Confederacy

(Continued from page 23)

It was evident from the beginning that Virginia would be the major battle ground of the war, and the State's famous Valley with its mountainous flanks had to be taken into consideration in any offensive or defensive plans of either the North or South.

It should be observed that while the Valley provided the best route for invasion from Virginia into the North, the reverse was not true, for an army following its course southwest would move away from rather than toward Richmond. However, in every campaign for the advance on Richmond the Union commanders had to guard against an attack on Washington by way of the Valley, and this fact enabled General Lee on several important occasions to keep the Northern armies divided over a wide territory.

But the town of the Valley which is the shrine of the South, and which attracts thousands of visitors from all over the country, is not the town in

which the greatest battle was fought, but that in which the Commander-in-Chief of the Confederate armies spent the last years of his life endeavoring to teach the young men of the South to be useful citizens of a reunited country. General Lee ennobled the position of college president by serving as the head of Washington College in Lexington from August, 1865, till his death on October 12, 1870.

The most cherished traditions of the University and of Lexington are associated with the life and personality of Robert Edward Lee. On the campus is the General's home, the Lee Chapel, built under his supervision, which contains the Lee Museum, his office preserved as he left it, and the recumbent statue of Lee by the eminent sculptor, Edward Valentine, late of Richmond. It is the stately simplicity and naturalness conveyed by this statue that impresses the visitor probably more than anything else in Lexington. In the crypt below the statue are the remains of General Lee, his father, "Light Horse Harry" Lee, and other members of his family.

The memory of General Stonewall Jackson is inseparably connected with the history of the Virginia Military Institute, where he served as Professor of Military Science and Natural Philosophy from 1852 till the beginning of the war. After his death at Chancellorsville, his body was brought to Lexington where he is honored today by a large bronze statue in the cemetery.

Matthew Fontaine Maury, the "Pathfinder of the Seas," to whom every ocean traveler is indebted, and a man especially honored by every important nation of the earth, supervised the coast defenses of the Confederacy, and after its fall became a member of the cabinet of the Emperor Maximilian in Mexico. He later returned to Lexington and served as a professor at the Virginia Military Institute for five years, until his death. A monument to his memory has been erected in the beautiful Goshen Pass, near Lexington, which he made forever famous by his dying request that his body be borne through it when the laurels were in bloom.

The rapid movements and brilliant strategy in General Jackson's famous Valley Campaign in the spring of 1862

will always interest the general reader as well as the student of military science. The campaigns, so ably executed by Jackson, should be remembered as a part of Lee's masterful plans for the defense of Richmond. As a part of his plan Lee ordered a vigorous offensive in the Valley to serve as a strategic diversion of the Federal troops to prevent the junction of the several Union armies under Banks, Fremont, McDowell, and McClellan. No abler man than General Jackson could have been chosen to execute such orders. After an earlier repulse

at Kernstown, in May Jackson moved forward vigorously and, by his rapid movements and skillfully planned attacks, entirely mystified the enemy and ultimately put them to flight, enabling himself to escape and go to the aid of Lee in defense of Richmond. Within a month he had marched 400 miles, fought six pitched battles, the most important of which was at Winchester on May 25, and captured thousands of prisoners and valuable supplies. In addition, he had not only prevented the union of the Federal armies but also had terrified the Fed-

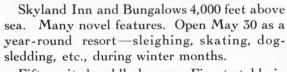

eral officials who made rapid plans for the defense of Washington which they thought was in immediate danger.

With the shifting of the scene of battle from Union territory to Virginia in 1864, the Valley was the scene of new combats. It was on May 15, 1864, that the "Charge of the Cadets," from the Virginia Military Institute, was made at New Market. While this charge had little effect on the outcome of the war, it will long be remembered because of the courageous heroism of the boys whose action is commemorated in an impressive ceremony held by their alma mater each year. Maj. Theodore S. Long, of the Federal commander's staff, wrote: "I must say that I have never witnessed a more gallant advance and final charge than was given by those brave boys on that field. They fought like veterans."

In June, Federal troops under General Hunter made a raid southward.

At Lexington, Governor Letcher's home and the buildings of the Virginia Military Institute were burned and the buildings of Washington College pillaged and damaged. In the same raid the Houdon statue of Washington was taken from the campus of the Institute, but it was restored after the war. Colonel Hayes and Major McKinley, of Hunter's command on this occasion, were afterwards Presidents of the United States. Hunter was forced westward by General Early, who now cleared the Valley of Federal troops and appeared at the very gates of Washington.

Meanwhile General Sheridan was ordered to the Valley, which he proceeded to make void of nearly everything which could be of immediate use to man or beast so that, according to his own boast, even a crow in flying over the country "would have to carry his own rations." No portion of the Valley became better known than

the region around Winchester, a town of important historical connections for nearly two hundred years, and where still are to be seen the houses used as headquarters by Generals Washington, Jackson, and Sheridan. It is said that during the war this town changed hands between the North and South seventy-two times, four times on one day. Through the entire length of the Valley Pike are to be found markers and monuments reminding the traveler of significant battles and events, most of which are connected with the War Between the States.

Petersburg's 300 Days
(Continued from page 55)

Gregg, that the signal gun was fired at 4:40 on the morning of April 2 for the general advance on Petersburg. This great stronghold was a key point and a turning point of Grant's long

line of forts stretching south and west of the city. Within these parapets and behind these bastions was space for an army. Fort Rice faced the Confederate line on the east of Petersburg with only two bastions to guard the Norfolk Railway, but here on the "western front" Fort Fisher faced the Confederate line to Hatcher's Run with four bastions.

OLD BLANDFORD CHURCH: The proper climax for the tour of the Petersburg lines is a visit to "Old Blandford" or Bristol Parish Church, the noblest shrine of them all. It is the Sainte Chapelle of the Confederacy. Built in 1735 and "standing in quiet beauty amid acres of heroic dust," it enshrines two centuries of history. Around its walls have surged the high tides of the life of the nation, for here Steuben's Virginia militia opposed the advance of the British under Phillips and Arnold in 1781, and here was the Cemetery Ridge at which Grant aimed in the Crater fight of 1864. The bloody lines of the Three Hundred Days barely missed these walls, and the fierce artillery fire of the Federal guns left traces on two of the adjacent monuments, the stately McRae monument to the Petersburg men of the War of 1812 and the simple shaft over the parson—grandfather of the writer.

Today the old church is a Confederate Memorial, a Pantheon of Confederate heroism. The mural tablets commemorate an early rector, a gallant leader, the Revolutionary patriots, the 9th of June men, the Crater Legion. Another tablet preserves the Virginia Elegy by a lesser Gray, "Thou art crumbling to the dust, old pile." But each of the eleven windows is a Tiffany Apostle window contributed and unveiled by a Confederate State to the glory of God and to the memory of her sons that fell here. The apostle of the Virginia window is Saint John, and the inscription is "Eternal right, though all else fail, can never be made wrong." Even the two "clerestory" windows are Maryland and Missouri memorials, and the arched window over the entrance is a memorial to the Ladies Memorial Association of Petersburg, the first in America.   *(See next page)*

(See next page)

It is a simple and impressive interior, with no traces of the panoply of war and no words of strife to mar the sacred precincts. Yet this seemly restraint has eloquence beyond words or symbols, this reverent silence voices "No reproach, no protest, no apology." The Three Hundred Days have passed into history, but not into the limbo of forgotten or unworthy deeds.

Defense and Defenders
(*Continued from page 27*)

was practically completed in 1845 and the name was changed to Fort Monroe. The post office, however, still bears the former title.

The only defense of the waters of Hampton, in the water itself, stands upon an artificial island called "Rip Raps" (a Danish noun). Its original name was Fort Calhoun, so designated to honor John C. Calhoun, of South Carolina. Its present name, changed in 1862, honored General Wool, a native of a Northern State.

During the war for Southern Independence the Confederates did not succeed in establishing any defenses on the north side of the James River below Mulberry Island. The Commonwealth, however, fortified the eastern side of the Elizabeth River by planting batteries on Sewall's Point (formerly Seawall's Point) while the guns on Bush's Bluff and at Lambert's Point were active at times.

This line has been recently located. Its right flank rested on the "Entrenchment Farm," the guns commanding the waters of Broad Creek, an extension of the Eastern Branch of the Elizabeth River; its left flank, distance about one and one-half miles, confronted any attack from the waters of Tanner's Creek.

Heavy works were constructed on Craney Island, on the western side of the Elizabeth River. General Lee's report mentioned that the Frigate *United States* "has been prepared for a school ship, provided with a deck battery of nineteen guns, thirty-two pounders and nine-inch Columbiads for harbor defense." The Confederates changed the name of this frigate to the *Confederate States*, and in 1862 she was stationed at the angle of the ship channel, near Craney Island, to obstruct the Federal men-of-war.

General Lee also relates that, "To prevent the ascent of the Nansemond River and the occupation of the railroad from Norfolk to Richmond, three batteries have been constructed on the river which will mount nineteen guns." Thus Lee, the greatest of American military strategists, realized early in the war the weakness of the situation caused by the determination to hold Richmond at the risk and final cost of crushing disaster.

The same vision saw the difficulty of supplying the defenders of the Nansemond by water, from Norfolk and Richmond. The swift, though small, C.S.S. *Roanoke* ran through the Union blockade from Norfolk to the Nansemond River, carrying subsistence and ammunition from Suffolk to the batteries on its bank and at its mouth, where it empties into the James.

The Defenders

The first defenders on the Peninsula during the War Between the States were Confederates at Little and Big Bethel, the opponents being troops from Fortress Monroe, whose greatest achievement was a blundering engagement in an action between themselves.

Commodore Matthew Fontaine Maury, whose devoted descendants will so fittingly honor his memory by the dedication of the starboard anchor of the C.S.S. *Virginia-Merrimac* on the lawn of the White House of the Confederacy during the Reunion, was in high place among the most distinguished defenders of the Commonwealth of his nativity.

His ardent devotion to the ideals of Old Virginia, his unselfish and unfailing labors, comes as one of the most pleasant chapters in the history of the Commonwealth. He gave to her cause all of his great knowledge of science, all of his skill, all of his powers for research, all of his genius for invention.

He early approved and supported the use of iron for armour; he was a supporter, not a critic, of the experimental *Virginia-Merrimac* as a defender of the great harbor of Virginia. He sensed the value for defense of submarine craft and submerged and floating mines, and was detached, too early, from special service in their construction and operation.

When it came to the Commodore's attention that there were nearly a score of wooden gunboats waiting in vain for their iron plating, he prepared a written proposal to the Confederate government urging the building of 100 steam launches, all of models suitable for "bay and river navigation only." Congress authorized the construction and Maury organized forces on the Virginia rivers where timber and experienced boatbuilders were available.

Under date of January 19, 1862, Commodore Maury wrote to Commodore William F. Lynch stressing the need for 100 lieutenants to command these boats and urging his assistance in securing and training the young officers.

This letter from Maury to Lynch was captured by the Federals and was reported by Flag Officer Golds-borough, U.S.N., from the U. S. Flagship *Philadelphia*, then off Roanoke Island, N. C., on February 14, 1862. Printed specifications of the steam gunboats alluded to by Maury were also captured.

The Secretary of the Navy in Richmond later secured the repeal of the act of Congress authorizing the construction of the 100 boats.

The Saga of Hampton Roads is not complete without a brief recital of the Federal defense and defenders of the waters of the great harbor of the Commonwealth. The abandonment of the Gasport Navy Yard was the most disgraceful episode in the history of the United States Navy. The U.S.S. steam frigate *Merrimac* was scuttled and sunk on the night of April 20, 1861. Her hull was raised by the Commonwealth, renamed the *Virginia*, and upon it was built a floating battery for harbor defense. The C.S.S. *Virginia-Merrimac* was the first and only vessel ever built with submerged decks, fore and aft, of an armored casement. She was armed with eight 9-inch Dahlgren smooth bores of the original battery of the U.S.S. *Merrimac*, and two 7-inch Brooke rifled pivot guns, the heaviest cannon in the world at the time.

A supply of U. S. Navy standard quality powder was found in the magazine of the old *Merrimac*. This supply was perfectly preserved and ample for use in her engagements of March 8-9, 1862. An inferior grade blasting powder was used in the shells fired from her guns. Coal for the *Virginia-Merrimac* was shipped from what is still known as the "Merrimac Mine" and was delivered on canal boats towed through the loosely guarded Federal blockade.

The *Virginia*, fortunately for the Federal government, was not covered with railroad rails, popular tradition

notwithstanding; fortunately, because plenty of rails were available and, if used would have enabled the Confederate government to employ the *Virginia* many months before her trial trip on March 8, 1862.

All preparations were made for the attack by the C.S.S. *Virginia-Merrimac* on the U.S. wooden sailing ships, *Congress* and *Cumberland*, anchored off Signal Point for months, to protect the flank of the Federal Army, then at Newport News. It was proposed to steam from Gosport on Thursday night, March 6.

The pilots on the *Virginia-Merrimac* protested after their alleged agreement to pilot her, and the attack was postponed until Saturday, March 8. The *Virginia-Merrimac** sank the *Cumberland*. (Her grave, unknown for nearly seventy years, has been determined with reasonable accuracy by the testimony of three men who assisted in the recovery of her anchor chain, now in Richmond.) Next the Confederate ironclad burned the *Congress*, three Federal frigates striving in vain to assist the doomed ship. The U.S.S. *Minnesota* reached the scene of action but grounded and was forced to cast some of her guns overside to lighten ship. Two other ships also grounded but escaped the heavy fire upon the *Minnesota* on March 8 and 9.

On Sunday, March 9, the *Virginia-Merrimac* and the *Monitor* were engaged for several hours. Only one man was seriously injured and little damage was done. A different story would have resulted had the *Monitor* used shells, with a full charge of powder, not one-half the standard charge; and had the *Virginia* used solid shot.

The location of the grave of the *Virginia-Merrimac*, destroyed by her commander when he found that Confederate troops had been withdrawn from the defense of Norfolk, without notice to him, has been fixed by recent research. The approximate spot has been determined (where the anchor was found), the same anchor to be dedicated to the memory of Commodore Matthew Fontaine Maury, the greatest figure in the naval history of the Confederacy.

*It is an historical error to refer to the *Virginia* as the *Merrimac*, since there was never a Confederate ship by that name. There were three craft in the Federal service named the *Merrimack*. Let all veterans use their individual influence to protest against the naming of the proposed National Marine Park area in Hampton Roads "The Merrimack and Monitor Park," as an inexcusable historical misnomer.

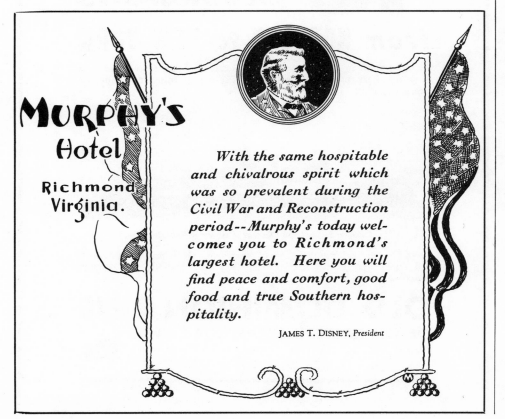

Objects of Confederate Interest in the Virginia State Library

(*Continued from page 43*)

note—written with a pencil—came into the State Library. This is a military paper of the Confederacy and, strictly speaking, probably be-

longs to the United States government. But it is not anticipated that the government will ever claim it.

There are other letters of Confederate officers to Governor Letcher, but none of special note. At one time there was in the Library a letter from Gen. George Thomas, at the time of the writing of which (March 12, 1861, before Virginia had seceded from the Union) he had not absolutely decided whether or not he would resign from the Union Army. This letter cannot now be found, but it is printed in full in the Calendar of Virginia State Papers.

There are in the Library a few relics of the War Between the States, the most interesting being probably the sword wielded by Maj. Heros von Borck, the immense German who served on Stuart's staff. It is about as large as that of the giant Revolutionary soldier, Peter Francisco, in the same display case.

The portrait of Gen. Robert E. Lee is one of the best portraits to be found of the great Southern leader. It was painted by the talented artist, John A. Elder, who also painted the Library's portrait of Joseph E. Johnston and that of Jubal A. Early. Of Gen. Robert E. Lee the Library has also a small full length plaster cast statue and it has an excellent bas-relief portrait bust by O'Donavan. Of Governor Smith it has a marble bust by E. V. Valentine. Of Governor Letcher it has a plaster bust by Alexander Galt. Of Stonewall Jackson it has a small plaster bust by Frederick Volck.

It has a portrait of President Jefferson Davis; also a bronze bust, by J. E. Miller. It has an excellent portrait of Commodore Maury, painted from life by John A. Elder, and a plaster bust made from life by E. V. Valentine. It has a portrait of Edmund Ruffin, who is said to have fired the first shot at Fort Sumter, and who has more enduring claims to fame on account of his articles on agricultural subjects, many of which were written for the *Farmers Register*. The Library has portraits of James Alexander Seddon, Secretary of War of the Confederate States, 1862-1865; Maj. W. T. Sutherlin, whose home in Danville was the

residence for some days (April 2-10) of Jefferson Davis after the evacuation of Richmond in 1865, and John R. Thompson, poet of the Confederacy. This portrait was painted by John A. Elder.

An example of John A. Elder's ideal painting, in which he excelled, is owned by the Library in the picture called "Appomattox," representing a Confederate soldier on his return home from Appomattox, having lost everything, but determined to carry on heroically to the last.

When John Gadsby Chapman died, C. W. Chapman presented to the Virginia State Library as a memorial all the paintings, etchings, and drawings left in his father's studio, a considerable number, and when C. W. Chapman died his widow did the

same thing with reference to her husband's effects, in this case, too, a considerable number. These have been prepared for exhibition by Mr. H. H. Harwood, an artist of skill and wide knowledge, and catalogued. They form a most attractive exhibit, much admired by visitors and sometimes closely studied. The subjects of the work of J. G. Chapman are largely Italian, but those of C. W. Chapman are largely Confederate.

Nearly all the governors of Virginia from the close of the War Between the States to a comparatively recent time and her other public men of distinction have been Confederate veterans.

The Library should be visited by all visitors to the city, especially at the time of the Confederate Reunion.

Women of the Confederacy
(Continued from page 26)

women of the Confederacy were denied.

Thirteen hundred Confederate soldiers passed through the Robertson Hospital in Richmond, passed under the rigid and close supervision of Captain Sally Tompkins, its founder and its guardian angel.

Captain Sally might organize better than anyone else, but there were thousands of women who had the healing touch, which wasn't really so much touch as the devotion to a country's cause behind it, which translated itself to the weary and often

despondent soldiers. Tillie Russell was one of these women. In 1864 when the Confederates had been engaged near Winchester in the Valley of Virginia and had been driven through the town, many wounded and dying lay untended on the field then held by the Federals. So numerous were the casualties that their surgeons could not attend to all.

A young Confederate, Randolph Ridgeley, suffered a fractured thigh and amputation was believed necessary, but the hard pressed surgeon, being unable to give immediate relief, passed on to other cases. Three days later a call for help in tending the sick was sent by a Confederate to

Dr. Love in Winchester. Twenty ladies responded and with them was Tillie Russell, an exceedingly attractive young girl. Standing near young Ridgeley she heard a doctor say as he passed, "That boy hasn't slept since the battle; he will die if he doesn't get some sleep." Tillie Russell's task was to save his life. Kneeling beside him she very tenderly lifted his head from its hard and knobby knapsack pillow until it rested comfortably on her arm. She smoothed his forehead and hummed a Southern song. Very soon the soldier slept quietly, and Tillie Russell, fearful lest the moving of a muscle should waken him, sat through the long cold night on the battlefield holding her wounded soldier.

Zora Fair was not called to minister upon a battlefield. She was a lovely and high bred girl who refugeed from Charleston to Dell Delight, near Covington in Georgia. From here she went out daily to wave to the carloads of Confederates that might pass through; she visited the improvised hospitals and attended the prayer services in the village church; but all this was so little, so little as to be nothing when one thought of the South in 1864.

The guns were pounding away at Atlanta when Zora decided to spy in Sherman's camp. Disguised as an old negress—her brown hair shorn and crimped, her skin stained with walnut juice—she set out on her forty-mile walk. The way was not easy; once she crossed the Yellow River by crawling over the charred timbers of a partially destroyed mill dam.

To the pickets around Atlanta she announced herself as "an ole nigger 'oman, looking for her husban' whar hed done run away to go wid Marse Sherman." She played her part convincingly, asking pathetically for her "ole man" until she reached headquarters where she begged to be allowed to speak to "Marse Gineral Sherman hisself." Finally allowed to wait in an ante room until the General had leisure to see her, she sat stupidly in a corner with her keen ears alert. From the conversation of Sherman and his officers in the adjoining room she learned of the plan to destroy Atlanta by fire, of the march to the sea and the intended siege of

Savannah. War was to be carried deep into the South and in its path would be Dell Delight.

Sherman did march to the sea and not the least precious of the things he crushed as he went was the heart of Zora Fair. Never strong, the rigors of her spying expedition and later of her exposure together with a sense of failure and grief over the desolation of her beautiful land were more than so slight a constitution could endure. She died not long before the Confederacy fell.

In the letters received by Governor John Letcher in April, 1861, shortly after Virginia's secession, is one written in a fine spidery hand on thin azure paper. It is from the ladies of Ingleside. One might have guessed its feminine authorship, but one would never guess correctly its contents. "Sir:" it reads, "Owing to our unprotected situation we are forced to call upon you for protection; husbands, brothers and sons have left for the field of battle determined upon *victory* or *death*. Not having a home guard, and living about seven miles from a place of protection, we have determined to protect our rights, our property and our homes. We ask you to consider our destitute situation and please send us half a dozen Colt's revolvers. They will be very thankfully received and most certainly used if necessary."

And finally there is the picture of Christmas, 1864: ". . . We were all busy preparing the tree for the children on Saturday before Christmas. It was beautiful! On top were two Confederate flags—our Confederate and our battle flags. General Lee, bless his soul, was hung immediately below." Tallow dips set in bottles were hidden in evergreens and Santa Claus left homemade toys —rag dolls whose cheeks were painted with poke berries and eyes with indigo and hair with sumach berries, and flutes made of lowland river reeds. The Christmas dinner was primarily a matter of rice and berries served in several styles, with wine, ground peas, apples, and, glory of glories, a cake made of dried cherries and whortle-berries, candied watermelon rind and sorghum!

Perhaps Stephen Vincent Benet has given us the most real picture of our gallant Southern lady:

The gentlemen killed and the gentlemen died,
But she was the South's incarnate pride
That mended the broken gentlemen
And sent them out to the war again;
That kept the house with the men away
And baked the bricks where there was no clay;
Made courage from terror and bread from bran
And propped the South on a swan's-down fan
Through four long years of ruin and stress,
The pride—and the deadly bitterness.

▲▲▲ RICHMOND, VIRGINIA ▲▲▲

Population—Metropolitan, 220,513; Corporate, 182,929, 15th Federal Census

Climate

A mild healthful climate, an average normal temperature of 57.7° F.;
No excessive summer heat;
A mean annual rainfall 41.73 inches;
Altitude from mean sea level to 235 feet;
A death rate of 12.63 per thousand population, 43% lower than in 1907.

Educational

A medical college with schools of medicine, dentistry, pharmacy and nursing;
A "University of Richmond," composed of Westhampton College for Women, Richmond College for Men, and T. C. Williams Law School (co-educational);
2 universities for colored students;
The Richmond Division of the College of William and Mary, including the School of Social Work and Public Health, the evening extension division and the day academic division;
The principal Presbyterian Theological Seminary in the South;
A Presbyterian Training School;
A city supported mechanical training school.

Financial

Banks' capital, surplus and undivided profits of $26,070,951.25;
Bank debits to individual accounts, $1,478,255,000.00;
Bank clearings of $1,748,565,238.62;
Bank resources of $150,126,717.15;
Bank deposits of $114,488,760.02;
Savings accounts totaling $46,113,521.28;
Federal Reserve Bank of the Fifth District, with Branches in Baltimore and Charlotte, N. C., employing 327 people in Richmond; Resources, $214,000,000; Cash Reserves, $101,000,000; Capital and Surplus, $17,000,000; Reserve Deposits, $47,000,000; handling 53,000,000 checks annually amounting to $10,000,000,000.

General

3 radio broadcasting stations;
A vast field of 1,152,000,000 tons of high grade free burning industrial coal within 15 miles of the city, extending through 190 miles and 5 counties;
An industrial power rate grading down to less than 1c per kilowatt hour;
A commercial gas rate graded from $1.30 to 55c per 1,000 cubic feet;
A water rate graduated according to consumption from 11c per 100 cubic feet to 5c per 100 cubic feet for all over 30,000 cubic feet;
216 churches, 17 denominations; 144 white and 72 colored.

Industrial

617 industrial organizations (including manufacturing) with capital of $276,628,992, and an annual output of $255,175,746;
302 MANUFACTURING plants using material valued at $82,880,-449.00, turning out products valued at $217,996,635.00. (1929- U. S. Census of Manufacturers.)
22 active industries in business here more than forty years.
416 wholesale and jobbing firms with net sales for 1929 of $233,611,053, employing 7,143 persons earning $11,219,791 annually.
2,570 retail stores with net sales for 1929 of $102,201,322, employing 10,607 persons earning $13,799,988 annually.

Transportation

A municipal airport—central operating base of New York, Richmond, Atlanta air mail route; daily passenger service North and South;
6 railroads; 2 steamship lines; 3 interurban electric lines;
15 passenger motor bus lines; 21 motor truck freight lines;
73 passenger buses arriving in city each day and 73 departing;
102 passenger trains arriving in and departing from the city daily;
Direct freight steamship service to and from New York;
Direct overnight steamship service to Newport News and Norfolk;

IV

"THE LAST PARADE"
by Douglas Southall Freeman

The Last Parade, by Douglas Southall Freeman, originally published in book form for private distribution
only in 1932, is reproduced in facsimile here through the
courtesy of Mrs. Leslie Cheek, Jr., the former Mary Tyler
Freeman, of Richmond. The 1932 printing was done with
french fold pages, unnumbered, with tipped-in illustrations and protective tissues for each photograph. Modern
printing methods have made it necessary in this edition
to omit certain blank pages that followed the photographs, but all pages appear in the order in which they
were originally published. The photographs are used
through the courtesy of Dementi-Foster Studios, Richmond, and are those from which the halftone illustrations
were made in 1932.

THE LAST PARADE

The
Last Parade

AN EDITORIAL BY
DOUGLAS S. FREEMAN

*From "Richmond News Leader" of Friday, June twenty-fourth
Nineteen hundred and thirty-two, the last day of
the forty-second annual reunion of the
United Confederate Veterans*

PUBLISHED BY
WHITTET & SHEPPERSON, RICHMOND, VA.
1932

THE LAST PARADE

THEY thronged the streets of this old town when Bonham brought his volunteers with their Palmetto flag in 1861. They cheered the lads who took up arms when first Virginia called. With doubtful glance they looked upon the men who hailed from New Orleans, the "Tigers" of the bayou state.

When Longstreet led his veterans from Centreville to hold the Yorktown line, all Richmond brought out food and flowers and draped the bayonets. When first the city heard the distant growl of Union guns, each regiment that came to strengthen Lee was welcomed as the savior of the South. The long procession of the carts that brought a groaning load across the Chickahominy from Gaines' Mill was watched with aching hearts.

"Many a fierce battle still lay before the Army of Northern Virginia; marvellous was the skill and audacity with which Lee manoueverd his ragged regiments in the face of over-whelming odds, but with Stonewall Jackson's death the impulse of victory died away."

—G. F. R. HENDERSON: *Stonewall Jackson.*

Another year and solemn strains and mourning drums received the train that had the silent form of him who was the "right arm" of his famous chief. That was the darkest day, save one, that Richmond ever knew, for when the "stonewall" fell, the stoutest bulwark of the South was down. With Jackson dead, where was another such?

When Pickett's soldiers came, a shattered fragment of defiant wrath, to tell how hell itself had opened on that hill at Gettysburg, the townsfolk gazed as if on men who had upturned their graves. The months that followed saw a steady flow into the mills of death. Each night the sleeping street was wakened by the tread of veterans who hurried on to meet the sullen Meade or hastened back to check the wily Sheridan. The clatter of the horses' hoofs, the rumble of the trains, the drum at dawn, the bugle on the midnight air—all these the leaguered city heard till children's talk was all of arms, and every chat across the garden wall was punctuated by the sound of fratricidal strife.

"Among the gallant soldiers who have fallen in this war General Stuart was second to none in valor, in zeal and in unfaltering devotion to his country. . . . To military capacity of a high order and all the nobler virtues of the soldier he added the brighter graces of a pure life, guided and sustained by the Christian's faith and hope."—*General Robert E. Lee's announcement to the Army of Northern Virginia, May 20, 1864, of the death of Major-General J. E. B. Stuart.*

Ten months of thunder and of ceaseless march and then the end. Brave Custis Lee led out the last defenders of the town, and limping Ewell rode away while flames leaped up and bridges burned and Trojan women waited death. The next parade was set to fastest time, as up the hill and past St. Paul's and in the gates the Federals rode and tore with wildest cheers the still-defiant flag from off the capitol. Dark orgy in the underworld and brutish plunder of the stores, a wider stretch of fire, the mad rejoicing of the slaves, the sly emergence of the spies; and after that the slow return of one gray rider through the wreck of fanes and dreams, a solitary horseman on a weary steed, with only youth and age to pay him homage as he stopped before his door and bowed to all and climbed the steps and went within and put aside his blade to work for peace.

Excited days of preparation then, and pontoons thrown across the James. The army of the victor, Grant, the gossips said, was soon to march through Richmond and to see the ashes of the pinnacles on which its dis-

"As for me, I speak only for myself; our Cause was so just, so sacred, that had I known all that has come to pass, had I known what was to be inflicted on me, all that my country was to suffer, I would do it again."

—*Jefferson Davis, addressing the Southern Historical Society.*

tant gaze had long been fixed. They came. In endless lines, all day they moved, all night, until the city's tearful folk became bewildered in their count and asked, How could the "thin, gray line" have stood so long against that host?

At last the blue-coats left and civil rule returned, in poverty and pain, but with a memory that made the humblest rich. The fallen walls were raised again, the peaceful smoke of busy trade rose where the battle-fumes had hung. For twenty years, the soldiers of the South remained behind the counter or the plow, until the day when Johnston led them out to lay the cornerstone of what the South designed to be a fit memorial to the matchless Lee. A few years more, and when the figure stood upon the pedestal, the word went out that every man who wore the gray should muster in the ranks again and pass before the chieftain on old Traveller. A day that was when love became the meat of life!

Reunions multiplied. A grateful city gladly threw its portals wide

LEE MONUMENT, RICHMOND, VIRGINIA

BIBLIOGRAPHICAL NOTE
AND INDEX

each time the aged survivors of Homeric strife returned to view the scenes of youth. A deep emotion rose as Forrest's troopers galloped past and Texans raised the "rebel yell." Today the city has its last review. The armies of the South will march our streets no more. It is the rear guard, engaged with death, that passes now. Who that remembers other days can face that truth and still withhold his tears? The dreams of youth have faded in the twilight of the years. The deeds that shook a continent belong to history. Farewell; sound taps! And then a generation new must face its battles in its turn, forever heartened by that heritage.

Bibliographical Note

The *Richmond Times-Dispatch* and *Richmond News Leader* for the period of the 1932 Confederate Reunion were indispensable for this book's text and illustrations. A scrapbook at the Museum of the Confederacy containing these newspapers enabled us to reproduce the numerous photographs from the original newsprint. Since all other files of the papers have been placed on microfilm, which does not reproduce well, the scrapbook at the museum was a godsend.

Three books were especially useful. William W. White's *The Confederate Veteran* (Tuscaloosa, Ala.: Confederate Publishing Co., 1962, Confederate Centennial Studies, No. 22) describes the activities of the former Confederate soldiers after the war, especially those of the United Confederate Veterans. It also recounts briefly the history of the Sons of Confederate Veterans, the United Daughters of the Confederacy, and the Children of the Confederacy. The book relates facts about the reunions held over the years and tells of the veterans' influence in politics. Curiously, it makes no mention of the final 1932 Reunion in Richmond or of the huge gathering that accompanied the unveiling of the Lee statue there in 1890. The even larger assemblage of veterans who attended the Jefferson Davis unveiling in 1907 is cited, but there is nothing concerning the J. E. B. Stuart unveiling a few days before.

Wallace Evan Davies's *Patriotism on Parade* (Cambridge, Mass.: Harvard Univ. Press, 1955) contains much interesting information concerning the activities of the United Confederate Veterans and the Grand Army of the Republic in the post-bellum years, the sometimes bitter controversies between them, attitudes in the North toward the South and vice versa, joint reunions of Northern and Southern veterans, President McKinley's conciliatory statements, criticism of the GAR for its raids on the U.S. Treasury, the violent objections of the GAR in 1897 to Grover Cleveland's attempt to return the captured Confederate battle-flags, and so on. The return of the flags in 1905 by unanimous joint resolution of Congress is related in *Southern Historical Society Papers* 32: 195–200 and 33: 297–305.

Paul H. Buck's *The Road to Reunion, 1865–1900* (Boston: Little, Brown, 1937) is an excellent, broadly sketched study of intersectional relations and their vicissitudes after the war. It quotes scathing statements by Northerners concerning the South's antebellum civilization, and describes the works of Southern writers in the postbellum era that gave a much more favorable picture. It relates how *Harper's Weekly* and the *Southern Review* each blasted attitudes on the other side of Mason and Dixon's Line, with *Harper's* later reversing its position. Southern woes during Reconstruction, conciliatory poems by Francis Miles Finch and James Russell Lowell, Northern aid to Southerners in the great yellow fever epidemic of 1878, the joint Gettysburg reunion of 1888, and the Force Bill's defeat in 1891 are all included.

Information as to Dan Emmett and his song "Dixie" was gathered from *Southern Historical Society Papers* 21: 212–14 and 36: 369–70. Data as to the origins of the term "Dixie" came from the 1981 edition of the *Encylopedia Americana*.

Various facts and sidelights concerning the Confederate reunions and dedications in Richmond are to be found in Virginius Dabney's *Virginia: The New Dominion* (Garden City, N.Y.: Doubleday, 1971) and *Richmond: The Story of a City* (Garden City, N.Y.: Doubleday, 1976).

Dixon Wecter's *When Johnny Comes Marching Home* (Boston: Houghton Mifflin, 1944) covers certain aspects of the North-South controversies after the war, and the activities of veterans. Beverley B. Munford's *Virginia's Attitude Toward Slavery and Secession* (Richmond: L. H. Jenkins, 1909) tells of the slaves owned, and in most cases not owned, by leading Virginia Civil War generals. W. Asbury Christian's *Richmond: Her Past and Present* (Richmond: L. H. Jenkins, 1912) is useful in pinpointing certain facts and dates.

Index

Names, Places, and Organizations cited in
The Last Review: A Memoir and *An Album of Photographs*

*—Indicates veteran at reunion.

*—Indicates veteran at reunion.

*—Indicates veteran at reunion.

This book was typeset in Bodoni Monotype and Linotype. It was printed on 60 pound Sebego Eggshell Oldstyle and 80 pound Warrens Lustro Offset Enamel in black and duotone process by Kingsport Press, Kingsport, Tennessee. It was bound in Arrestox C by Kingsport Press. The design is by Anne Theilgard of Joyce Kachergis Book Design & Production of Bynum, North Carolina. It was produced by Joyce Kachergis Book Design & Production.